The Right Course and the Only Right Choice

Jesus, Savior, Pilot Me Over Life's Tempestuous Sea

James Perry

The Right Course and the Only Right Choice

Published by:
Theocentric Publishing Group
1069 Main Street
Chipley, Florida 32428

http://www.theocentricpublishing.com

ISBN 9780984570898

A DEDICATION

Over the years, there have been several people who have had an impact in my life - - -

A 3rd and 4th Grade school-teacher who saw some potential in me and was a regular encouragement...

A man who worked for the Department of Sanitation in New York City who made it a point to not let me fall through the cracks...

After I was enrolled in College - - -

There was a lady who went to her church each day and lit a candle and prayed for me...

There was a lady of meager means who sent $5.00 per month to help with my schooling – and - prayed regularly for me...

After I became a Pastor - - -

A man who prayed, that as I served the Lord, I would show neither fear nor favor toward man...

I am indebted to each of these – Mrs. Halloren; Mr. Miller; Mrs. Ilardi; Mrs. Garrison; Mr. Grosshans - and many others, who

nudged me at the right time that I might find my potential and achieve exploits for the Lord.
May their tribe increase.

Psalm 145:3-4
Great is the Lord, and greatly to be praised, and His greatness is unsearchable. One generation shall commend your works to another, and shall declare your mighty acts.

Foreword

When travelling, one has a particular destination in view. During that journey, it's invaluable to have Rest Areas and Welcome Centers along the way - to be able to look at a Map hung on the wall, with a clear indicator, "You Are Here!"

It's important to know where one is going and the best way to get there. The words of Thomas in John 14:5, "...Lord, we do not know where you are going. How can we know the way?" Clear direction is needed.

It is hoped that in this study we will (a) become better acquainted with The One Who is our Guide; (b) gain insight in terms of the journey and what it entails; (c) be wary of the dangers and pitfalls along the way; and (d) to grow in confidence that The Guide – Jesus Christ – knows the way through the wilderness – all one has to do is follow Him and be assured of arriving at the destination safely.

Table of Contents

Great Expectation

Many are familiar with the classic novel by Charles Dickens entitled Great Expectations. It is the story of the orphan Pip from the days of his early childhood until adulthood and his effort to try to be a gentleman along the way. The story begins on Christmas Eve 1812 when Pip is 7 years old and continues through to the winter of 1840. It moves through various stages of experiences and expectations in Pip's life.

In anyone's life, there is always the personal expectation – schooling, career, marriage, family, etc. It serves as a goal and motivation as one navigates through the un-chartered waters of life. Expectation is an "eager anticipation: something expected: prospects, especially of success or gain." Sadly, some people have been reared in a context of low expectations, either for themselves or for others. It is like a negative echo-chamber – "you'll never amount to anything!"...or, "what makes you think you can succeed/achieve?"

Perhaps this is an analysis that can be applied to the Susan Boyle phenomena (April 11, 2009) and the tremendous response to this ordinary person following her appearance on Britain's Got Talent. Some of the explanation about this event is revealing...An article in USA Today (April 20, 2009) is entitled: "Why Susan Boyle Inspires Us." An explanation given is: "Boyle, for those who have been unconscious lately, is the middle-aged woman with frizzy hair who has been all over TV and computer screens for days, singing a Broadway show tune while millions wept and shouted and applauded wildly. Ten days ago, Boyle - 47, unglamorous, unfashionable, unknown - faced down a sneering British audience and panel of judges on Britain's Got

Talent...Then, in an instant, she turned jeers to cheers with her rendition of one of the weepier numbers from Les Misérables...All of us reveled in the fact that even in our image-managed world, we could still have the tables turned on us...Last week, Susan Boyle was on TV from early morning to late night, telling her Cinderella back story (youngest of nine, learning-disabled and bullied as a child, caretaker for her dying mother, never been kissed, singer in the choir, possessor of big dreams) to all who trekked in person or by satellite to her Scottish village outside Edinburgh..."

Some of the other random comments made were: "Every time I watched it, I felt emotional," says Julie Carrigan, 47, a mother of five in Hemet, Calif. But why? It's the vindication. "When they were making fun of her, I was getting annoyed...And inside I'm thinking, 'I hope she blows them away.' I was so happy when she just let them have it." It's the surprise. "If you have expectations of someone, you need to be prepared to be surprised by them," says Paul Potts..."It's part of human nature to make judgments based on first impressions, but sometimes we allow ourselves to be misguided by first impressions." It's the guilt. Why the surprise? There's no correlation between appearance and talent, says Scott Grantham..."If she didn't look the way she did, would there be the same reaction? I don't think so," he says. "We make snap judgments based on appearance, and when we see those judgments were premature, we over-compensate by going so far in the other direction." It's the shame. Boyle forced people to recognize how often they dismiss or ignore people because of their looks. "Is Susan Boyle ugly? Or are we?" asked essayist Tanya Gold in Britain's The Guardian.

The best summary may be: "For many, it all comes down to ancient wisdom." Rahn Hasbargen, an accountant in St. Paul, cites John 7:24: "Do not judge according to appearance, but judge with righteous judgment." "Never has that verse been explained more dramatically than in the case of Susan Boyle…" The Epistle of James, chapter 2, underscores this thought and echoes God's Law in Leviticus 19:15-18, "Always judge your neighbors fairly, neither favoring the poor nor showing deference to the rich…Do not try to get ahead at the cost of your neighbor's life, for I am the Lord. Never…bear a grudge against anyone, but love your neighbor as yourself. I am the Lord." We also note from Romans 15:7 that which should be the common practice, especially of God's people, namely, "Accept one another, then, just as Christ accepted you, in order to bring praise to God." Acceptance rather than Judgment – what a tremendous challenge and opportunity!

When Jesus began calling men to follow Him, His Call was simple, clear and direct. In Matthew 4:18-22, "While walking by the Sea of Galilee, he saw two brothers, Simon (who is called Peter) and Andrew his brother, casting a net into the sea, for they were fishermen. And he said to them, Follow me, and I will make you fishers of men. Immediately they left their nets and followed him. And going on from there he saw two other brothers, James the son of Zebedee and John his brother, in the boat with Zebedee their father, mending their nets, and he called them. Immediately they left the boat and their father and followed him." These verses are filled with expectation – the expectation of Jesus as He issued the call, and the expectation of those He called that they would become more than what the were and had been.

The Call:
Follow Me!
I will make you fishers of men!

The Response:
Immediately they left the boat and their father
They followed Him.

Later, this call would be reiterated and amplified. In Matthew 11:28-30, where Jesus said, "Come to me, all who labor and are heavy laden, and I will give you rest. Take my yoke upon you, and learn from me, for I am gentle and lowly in heart, and you will find rest for your souls. For my yoke is easy, and my burden is light." Note what is included - - -

Take My yoke upon you...One is not on his own with the latitude of doing whatever one wants, whenever one wants. It means being controlled and teamed with another or others.

Learn from me (and learn about Me). The desire to learn the ways and will of the Lord

Jesus says, I am gentle and lowly in heart. The need to function and do ministry as Jesus did it. Not being in it or doing it for bragging rights, but being a humble and faithful servant.

This is further evidenced in the ministry of the Apostles and the emerging Church. The Apostle Paul was careful to establish a standard, goal and expectation for his life, as well as for the lives of the believers. In Acts 20:22-25, his personal expectation and readiness is expressed:

"And now, behold, I am going to Jerusalem, constrained by the Spirit, not knowing what will happen to me there, except that the Holy Spirit testifies to me in every city that imprisonment and afflictions await me. But I do not account my life of any value nor as precious to myself, if only I may finish my course and the ministry that I received from the Lord Jesus, to testify to the gospel of the grace of God. And now, behold, I know that none of you among whom I have gone about proclaiming the kingdom will see my face again." Paul is allowing that there can be persecution aimed at those who proclaim the Gospel of the Lord Jesus Christ. The reaction and response to the Gospel can be vile and vicious.

The Book of Revelation gives a glimpse of those who have suffered for the sake of the Gospel. Revelation 6:9-10, "When he opened the fifth seal, I saw under the altar the souls of those who had been slain for the word of God and for the witness they had borne. They cried out with a loud voice, O Sovereign Lord, holy and true, how long before you will judge and avenge our blood on those who dwell on the earth?" They are desiring the Day of Vengeance of our God.

In Revelation 20:4 are these words: "Then I saw thrones, and seated on them were those to whom the authority to judge was committed. Also I saw the souls of those who had been beheaded for the testimony of Jesus and for the word of God, and those who had not worshiped the beast or its image and had not received its mark on their foreheads or their hands. They came to life and reigned with Christ..."

A similar picture is drawn in Hebrews 11:35-38, "...But others trusted God and were tortured, preferring to die rather than turn from God and be free. They placed their hope in the resurrection to a better life. Some were mocked, and their backs were cut open with whips. Others were chained in dungeons. Some died by stoning, and some were sawed in half; others were killed with the sword. Some went about in skins of sheep and goats, hungry and oppressed and mistreated. They were too good for this world. They wandered over deserts and mountains, hiding in caves and holes in the ground…"

Paul is enjoining the followers of Christ to remain faithful and to finish well – regardless of the personal cost. In Philippians 1:19-21, he validates and echoes this same aspiration:

"…for I know that through your prayers and the help of the Spirit of Jesus Christ this will turn out for my deliverance, as it is my eager expectation and hope that I will not be at all ashamed, but that with full courage now as always Christ will be honored in my body, whether by life or by death. For to me to live is Christ, and to die is gain."

The standard for the Church at Philippi is no different. In Philippians 1:27-28, he shares and challenges the fellow-believers: "Only let your manner of life be worthy of the gospel of Christ, so that whether I come and see you or am absent, I may hear of you that you are standing firm in one spirit, with one mind striving side by side for the faith of the gospel, and not frightened in anything by your opponents. This is a clear sign to them of their destruction, but of your salvation, and that from God." Paul is sharing thoughts about the obvious, namely, life is marked by uncertainties and unknowns. He challenges the followers of Christ to be completely focused on the character of God for and in their lives, as well as being committed to the task and doing it wholeheartedly. While the yoke of Jesus Christ may be easy and the burden may be light, the opposition can be very fierce and harsh. They will be relentless in their effort to silence the message and messengers of the Gospel. That's a reason why Paul stated in Romans 8:18-21 (NIV) - - -

"I consider that our present sufferings are not worth comparing with the glory that will be revealed in us. The creation waits in eager expectation for the sons of God to be revealed. For the creation was subjected to frustration, not by its own choice, but by the will of the one who subjected it, in hope that the creation itself will be liberated from its bondage to decay and brought into the glorious freedom of the children of God." When Paul says: "the creation waits in eager expectation...," he is referring to that time when it will be liberated from bondage, decay and oppression. The Message Paraphrase of Romans 8:18-21 expresses it: "That's why I don't think there's any comparison between the present hard times and the coming good times. The created world itself can hardly wait for what's coming next. Everything in creation is being more or less held back. God reins it in until both creation and all the creatures are ready and can be released at the same moment into the glorious times ahead. Meanwhile, the joyful anticipation deepens..."

The Church at Philippi receives another word of caution and encouragement in Philippians 3:18-21(ESV), "For many, of whom I have often told you and now tell you even with tears, walk as enemies of the cross of Christ. Their end is destruction, their god is their belly, and they glory in their shame, with minds set on earthly things. But our citizenship is in heaven, and from it we await a Savior, the Lord Jesus Christ, who will transform our lowly body to be like his glorious body, by the power that enables him even to subject all things to himself." It will be a day of grand and glorious liberty for all who have faithfully followed and served.

In 1877, Frances R. Havergal wrote the words to a very stirring and challenging Hymn.

Great Expectation

Who is on the Lord's side? Who will serve the King?
Who will be His helpers, other lives to bring?
Who will leave the world's side? Who will face the foe?
Who is on the Lord's side? Who for Him will go?
By Thy call of mercy, by Thy grace divine,
We are on the Lord's side—Savior, we are Thine!

Not for weight of glory, nor for crown and palm,
Enter we the army, raise the warrior psalm;
But for love that claimeth lives for whom He died:
He whom Jesus nameth must be on His side.
By Thy love constraining, by Thy grace divine,
We are on the Lord's side—Savior, we are Thine!

Fierce may be the conflict, strong may be the foe,
But the King's own army none can overthrow;
'Round His standard ranging, victory is secure,
For His truth unchanging makes the triumph sure.
Joyfully enlisting, by Thy grace divine,
We are on the Lord's side—Savior, we are Thine!

Personal Study Questions - - -

Do you believe Christ's Call to "Come" was just for the 12 disciples, or is it a Call for you as well? Explain!

When Jesus issued the subsequent "Call" in Matthew 11:28-30, was that a "Call" to you or to a limited and specific group He was addressing in His day? Why?

Do you believe that all of God's Children are "disciples" and must learn from following Christ?

In Hebrews 11, where do you believe you "fit" (if the list was expanded to include our current times)?

May the Lord enable you to follow Him victoriously!
May you find Joy as you follow Jesus!

Great Gift

But now that you have been set free from sin and have become slaves of God, the fruit you get leads to sanctification and its end, eternal life. For the wages of sin is death, but the free gift of God is eternal life in Christ Jesus our Lord.
Romans 6:22-23

Most people have had the experience of receiving various gifts from time to time – for a Birthday, Graduation, Anniversary, some special accomplishment – given and received as a memento or reward to assist one in remembering the special occasion. If you tried to recall the gifts you have been given, would you be able to remember them all? Those that you could remember, can you remember why they were given? Do you think this is either a consequence or fulfillment of the Dutch Proverb that we get: "Too Soon Old and Too Late Smart"? Dr. Gordon Livingston has written a book with that title. He lists 31 essential truths for life. A reviewer states: "He writes from the premise that even though we can't escape who we are or what has happened to us, we are still in control of who we would like to become and what we want to accomplish." That's an interesting conclusion inasmuch as one of Dr. Livingston's Chapters and Summary is: "Life's two most important questions are 'Why?' and 'Why not?' The trick is knowing which one to ask. Understanding why we do certain things is the first step to change."

Wikipedia has the following and interesting background material about a well-known story and gift. "The Greatest Gift is a 1943 short story written by Philip Van Doren Stern which became the basis for the film It's a Wonderful Life. The story begins during the Holiday with George Pratt, a man who is unsatisfied with his life and ready to commit suicide, standing on a bridge. A strange, shabbily-dressed and well-mannered man approaches him, carrying a satchel. The man strikes up a conversation and George tells the man that he wishes he had never been born. The man tells him that his wish has been made official and that he was never born. The man tells George that he should take the satchel with him and pretend to be a door-to-door brush salesman when he sees anyone. When George returns home, he does as he is told and is shocked to discover that not only does his wife not know him, everyone who knew him took different and often negative steps in life because George had never been born - including his little brother, who he had saved in a pond accident and instead had died without George to save him. George offers his wife a complimentary upholstery brush, which she takes, and then he leaves the house after his wife's new husband tells him to leave. Upon his departure, his wife's son pretends to shoot him with a fake cap gun and shouts, You're dead. Why won't you die? George returns to the bridge and questions the man, who explains to him that he wanted more when he had already been given the greatest gift of all - the gift of life. George, now realizing the lesson, begs the man to return the gift of life and the man agrees to it. George returns home to check if the man did, in fact, change everything back to normal. Sure enough, everything is normal and he hugs his wife, and explains that he thought he had lost her. She is confused, and as he is about to explain everything, when his hand bumps a brush on the sofa behind him. Without turning around, George knows the brush was the one he had presented to her earlier."

The historical background states: "Inspired by a dream, Stern wrote a 4,100-word short story called The Greatest Gift in

1943 after working on it since the late 1930s. Unable to find a publisher, he sent the 200 copies he had printed as a 21-page booklet to friends as Christmas presents in December 1943. The story came to the attention of RKO Pictures producer David Hempstead, who showed it to actor Cary Grant, who was interested in playing the lead role. RKO purchased the motion-picture rights for $10,000 in April 1944. After several screenwriters worked on adaptations, RKO sold the rights to the story in 1945 to Frank Capra's production company for the same $10,000, which he adapted into It's a Wonderful Life. The story was first published as a book in December 1944, with illustrations by Rafaello Busoni. Stern also sold it to Reader's Scope magazine, which published the story in its December 1944 issue, and also to the magazine Good Housekeeping, which published it under the title The Man Who Was Never Born in its January 1945 issue..."

Watching the old film, "It's A Wonderful Life", has become a yearly tradition and is shown frequently during the Christmas period. While the film allows one a mushy response, it also has a subtle message attached to it, namely, Secular Humanism. What is the objective of the Secular Humanist? In 1930, Charles F. Potter wrote and published, "Humanism: A New Religion" with the summation that indicated: "Secular Humanism is an attempt to function as a civilized society with the exclusion of God and His moral principles." The Secular Humanists are patient, as well as subtle. They are somewhat like the woodsman attempting to split a log. He will tap his wedge into what he deems is a vulnerable spot. If it is met with resistance, he will move his wedge and try to penetrate from a different spot. At some point, the resistance to the wedge and the pounding by the sledge – the log will yield and begin to split. That's the way it is with the philosophy and principles of Humanism and other erroneous viewpoints. Patiently pounding away; approaching from a different angle; never stop trying – until there is less resistance and final succumbing when the log finally yields and splits.

No one would deny that "Life" is an invaluable gift! The issue is that "Life" does not exist in a vacuum. To define the word – "life" – is an interesting exercise. The Online Dictionary lists 36 possible definitions; the World English Dictionary lists 33 possibilities; plus submissions offered by the Medical and Scientific Dictionaries. A primary definition for "life" is: "the condition that distinguishes organisms from inorganic objects and dead organisms, being manifested by growth through metabolism, reproduction, and the power of adaptation to environment through changes originating internally."

Biblically, life is a Creation of God. He breathed into the nostrils of man, and man became a living soul. The Bible discusses life in general ways – both physical and spiritual. The Physical - Psalm 90:10-13 (ESV – Selected): "The years of our life are seventy, or even by reason of strength eighty; yet their span is but toil and trouble; they are soon gone, and we fly away...So teach us to number our days that we may get a heart of wisdom. Return, O Lord! How long? Have pity on your servants!"

We glean another reflection about life in Psalm 139:7-17 (ESV – Selected): "Where shall I go from your Spirit? Or where shall I flee from your presence?...If I say, Surely the darkness shall cover me, and the light about me be night, even the darkness is not dark to you; the night is bright as the day, for darkness is as light with you. For you formed my inward parts; you knitted me together in my mother's womb. I praise you, for I am fearfully and wonderfully made...My frame was not hidden from you, when I was being made in secret, intricately woven in the depths of the earth. Your eyes saw my unformed substance; in your book were written, every one of them, the days that were formed for me, when as yet there was none of them. How precious to me are your thoughts, O God! How vast is the sum of them!"

A more earthy statement about life is given in James 4:13-17 (Selected): "Come now, you who say, Today or tomorrow we will go into such and such a town and spend a year there and trade and make a profit - yet you do not know what tomorrow will bring. What is your life? For you are a mist that appears for a little time and then vanishes...you ought to say, If the Lord wills, we will live and do this or that. As it is, you boast in your arrogance..."

When one focuses on the Spiritual, there is a more full dimension of life given. In I John 5:11-13 - "And this is the testimony, that God gave us eternal life, and this life is in his Son. Whoever has the Son has life; whoever does not have the Son of God does not have life. I write these things to you who believe in the name of the Son of God that you may know that you have eternal life." This is as clear cut and plain as it can be!

When Jesus is praying, He emphasizes in John 17:3 - "And this is eternal life, that they know you the only true God, and Jesus Christ whom you have sent." Jesus amplifies defines "eternal life" for us.

One needs to ponder the words of I John 5:11, "...God gave us eternal life, and this life is in His Son..." Obviously, this is the greatest of any gift that can be given and received. It has its origin in eternity and is valid for all eternity. God's Great Gift to and for us is not deserved; it cannot be earned; and it cannot be purchased by man. He gave us His Son! We read about this gift in John 3:16-18 - "For God so loved the world, that he gave his only Son, that whoever believes in him should not perish but have eternal life. For God did not send his Son into the world to condemn the world, but in order that the world might be saved through him. Whoever believes in him is not condemned, but whoever does not believe is condemned already, because he has not believed in the name of the only Son of God."

God's Great Gift was planned for us – before our birth; before we had done anything good or bad; before creation occurred. This gift is disclosed and discussed in I Peter 1:17-21 - "And if you call on him as Father who judges impartially according to each one's deeds, conduct yourselves with fear throughout the time of your exile, knowing that you were ransomed from the futile ways inherited from your forefathers, not with perishable things such as silver or gold, but with the precious blood of Christ, like that of a lamb without blemish or spot. He was foreknown before the foundation of the world but was made manifest in the last times for the sake of you who through him are believers in God, who raised him from the dead and gave him glory, so that your faith and hope are in God."

The idea of "when" this gift was planned dispels the notion that any intrinsic good or good works was a determining factor in terms of "who" would be a recipient of this great gift. The bottom-line is that it is all of and from God. This is evidenced in Romans 9:8-16, "This means that it is not the children of the flesh who are the children of God, but the children of the promise are counted as offspring. For this is what the promise said: About this time next year I will return, and Sarah shall have a son. And not only so, but also when Rebekah had conceived children by one man, our forefather Isaac, though they were not yet born and had done nothing either good or bad - in order that God's purpose of election might continue, not because of works but because of him who calls - she was told, The older will serve the younger. As it is written, Jacob I loved, but Esau I hated. What shall we say then? Is there injustice on God's part? By no means! For he says to Moses, I will have mercy on whom I have mercy, and I will have compassion on whom I have compassion. So then it depends not on human will or exertion, but on God, who has mercy."

It is important for one to grasp the motivation behind this great gift given by God. The opening words of John 3:16 express it clearly - "God so loved." Anything made available and given by God to us is based upon His love, mercy and grace. In I Corinthians 13:13, the teaching on what love is, Paul concludes that chapter with these words: "So now faith, hope, and love abide, these three; but the greatest of these is love." In a similar way, Jude concludes his brief epistle that summarizes the perilous end times with these words: "But you must remember, beloved, the predictions of the apostles of our Lord Jesus Christ. They said to you, In the last time there will be scoffers, following their own ungodly passions. It is these who cause divisions, worldly people, devoid of the Spirit. But you, beloved, building yourselves up in your most holy faith and praying in the Holy Spirit, keep yourselves in the love of God, waiting for the mercy of our Lord Jesus Christ that leads to eternal life. And have mercy on those who doubt; save others by snatching them out of the fire; to others show mercy with fear, hating even the garment stained by the flesh." The emphasis is - - -

1. build yourselves up in your most holy faith
2. keep yourselves in the love of God,
3. wait for the mercy of our Lord Jesus Christ that leads to eternal life.

While one is waiting for the mercy of God, there needs to be a display of that same mercy - "...have mercy on those who doubt..." and "...to others show mercy with fear..." Always rejoice because of the love, mercy and grace God has shown you. Always be eager to share that same message of hope – the love, mercy and grace of God – with all others.

Personal Study Questions - - -

If someone asked you a reason for the hope that is in you, what would you say?

Are there some people who are unworthy to hear about the love. mercy and grace of God? Who are they? Why are they unworthy?

Write out a brief and simple presentation of the Gospel. Is it entirely Biblical? Is it clear?

A Practical Tool for sharing the Gospel is The Roman Road – A Plan of Salvation. The Roman Road to Salvation is a way of explaining the good news of salvation using verses from the Book of Romans. It is a simple yet powerful method of explaining why we need salvation, how God provided salvation, how we can receive salvation, and what are the results of salvation.

The first verse on the Romans Road to salvation is - Romans 3:23, "For all have sinned, and come short of the glory of God." The Bible states we have all sinned. We have all done things that are displeasing to God. There is no one who is innocent. Romans 3:10-18 gives a detailed picture of what sin looks like in our lives.

The second Scripture on the Romans Road to salvation, Romans 6:23, teaches us about the consequences of sin – "For the wages of sin is death; but the gift of God is eternal life through Jesus Christ our Lord." The punishment that we have earned for our sins is death. Not just physical death, but eternal death!

The third verse on the Romans Road to salvation picks up where Romans 6:23 left off - "but the gift of God is eternal life through Jesus Christ our Lord." Romans 5:8 declares, "But God demonstrates His own love toward us, in that while we were still sinners, Christ died for us." Jesus' death paid for the price of our sins. Jesus' resurrection proves that God accepted Jesus' death as the payment for our sins.

The fourth stop on the Romans Road to salvation is Romans 10:9, "that if you confess with your mouth Jesus as Lord, and believe in your heart that God raised Him from the dead, you will be saved." Because of Jesus' death on our behalf, all we have to do is believe in Him, trusting His death as the payment for our sins - and we will be saved! Romans 10:13 says it again, "for everyone who calls on the name of the Lord will be saved." Jesus died to pay the penalty for our sins and rescue us from eternal death. Salvation, the forgiveness of sins, is available to anyone who will trust in Jesus Christ as their Lord and Savior.

The final aspect of the Romans Road to salvation is the re-sults of salvation. Romans 5:1 - "Therefore, since we have been justified through faith, we have peace with God through our

Lord Jesus Christ." Through Jesus Christ we can have a relationship of peace with God. Romans 8:1 - "Therefore, there is now no condemnation for those who are in Christ Jesus." Because of Jesus' death on our behalf, we will never be condemned for our sins.

Finally, we have this precious promise of God from Romans 8:38-39, "For I am convinced that neither death nor life, neither angels nor demons, neither the present nor the future, nor any powers, neither height nor depth, nor anything else in all creation, will be able to separate us from the love of God that is in Christ Jesus our Lord."

Would you like to follow the Romans Road to salvation? Would you like to ask Jesus Christ to be your Savior and Lord right now?

If so, then pray this prayer - "God, I know that I have sinned against you and am deserving of punishment. I confess my sins to You and repent. I place my trust in You for salvation. I want to be a new creature in Jesus Christ. Thank You for Your wonderful grace and forgiveness - Your gift of eternal life in Christ! Amen!"

Great Rejection

For the wrath of God is revealed from heaven against all ungodliness and unrighteousness of men, who by their unrighteousness suppress the truth. For what can be known about God is plain to them, because God has shown it to them. For his invisible attributes, namely, his eternal power and divine nature, have been clearly perceived, ever since the creation of the world, in the things that have been made. So they are without excuse.
Romans 1:18-20

Romans 1 is a definitive chapter in God's Word. Paul is very clear about the urgency of the Gospel; his personal commitment to the Gospel; and his determination to make the Gospel known to all. Note the commitment and intensity as he states it in Romans 1:14-17 -

First: "I am under obligation both to Greeks and to barbarians, both to the wise and to the foolish." Paul is sharing his sense that he has a moral and legal obligation to make the Gospel known to all in the known world. It was given to him by God's calling of him. He intends to be careful and diligent to fulfill this obligation without delay.

Second: "So I am eager to preach the gospel to you also who are in Rome." The word "so" can be appropriately shifted so the verse will read: "I am so eager to preach the Gospel to you..." This is not a duty he regrets but one that fills him with anticipation, eagerness and excitement as he contemplates the privilege that has been entrusted to him, namely, the Gospel without borders or restriction.

Third: "For I am not ashamed of the gospel, for it is the power of God for salvation to everyone who believes, to the Jew first and also to the Greek." The compelling force within and the constant motivation of Paul has a singular measuring point, namely, "I am not ashamed…"

Jesus spoke of the seriousness of being ashamed of Him and His Gospel. Note what He says in Mark 8:34-38, "When He had called the people to Himself, with His disciples also, He said to them, Whoever desires to come after Me, let him deny himself, and take up his cross, and follow Me. For whoever desires to save his life will lose it, but whoever loses his life for My sake and the gospel's will save it. For what will it profit a man if he gains the whole world, and loses his own soul? Or what will a man give in exchange for his soul? For whoever is ashamed of Me and My words in this adulterous and sinful generation, of him the Son of Man also will be ashamed when He comes in the glory of His Father with the holy angels." It is difficult to visualize anyone choosing to ignore the appeal and stipulation by Jesus Christ. To follow Christ means:

- Desiring to come after Jesus
- Denying himself – herself in the process
- Taking up his/her cross (daily) - and -
- Following Jesus Christ from that moment forward.

It will take this kind of commitment to make it to the finish line. It will involve a clear calculation – profit versus loss. The profit equals gaining the whole world; the loss is losing one's soul. It will also include a determination regarding Christ and His Words. It echoes the words of Jesus in John 15, namely, the one desiring God abiding in Christ and His Words abiding within the individual. Mark 8:38 is abundantly clear – if anyone is ashamed of Jesus Christ and His Word in deference to the "adulterous and sinful generation" – then the Son of Man will be ashamed of that one when He comes again. To be ashamed in this sense is to have regret and remorse. Can one begin to imagine the anguish of Jesus Christ when he regrets and has remorse over one who professed to be His very own. As a parent, my goal and hope was that my children would never be shamed by anything I did. In a reciprocal way, I wanted them to know that their behavior and choices could and would bring shame to their parents. If earthly parents can have that sense and possible pain, how much more must the Lord Jesus Christ have that sense and pain when a professing child of God brings both reproach and shame to His name.

Anyone who attended an Evangelism Explosion Seminar with Dr. D. James Kennedy will remember the dramatic illustration he used about a young soldier in the army of Alexander the Great. In summary, those who had shown cowardice in battle had to appear before their great leader. One by one, those who had been guilty of cowardice were sentenced to immediate execution. As the young solder approached Alexander the Great, the great leader felt compassion toward the young soldier. What is your name, young man? He answered – Alexander! What did you say your name was? Alexander, sir! Then Alexander the Great declared: Young man – either change your behavior or change your name! That's the general idea of Mark 8:34-38. If one doesn't change his/her behavior as a "Christian", then Christ will be ashamed and the so-called "Christian" will come under the pending judgment. Its either (a) change your behavior, or (b) change your name.

There is another vital thought shared by Paul in Romans 1:17 regarding the Gospel, "For in it the righteousness of God is revealed from faith for faith, as it is written, The righteous shall live by faith." For the one assuming the duty and obligation of making the Gospel known; and the one eagerly committed to whatever is entailed to fulfill that obligation; and the one who is not ashamed of the Gospel – if one has embraced the Gospel, then one has embraced how one should live – namely: "The just (righteous) shall live by faith." When Paul sets down these markers for evangelism and the message of the Gospel, he has already experienced the reality of "it is the power of God unto salvation, to everyone who believes, to the Jew first and also to the Gentile."

With that kind of energy and dynamic appeal, one would think that it would have great appeal and result for all those hearing the Gospel. However, within the context of Romans 1, that is not the case. There are those who will resist and reject the things of God, as well as the Gospel of the Lord Jesus Christ. The words under the title of this chapter are a succinct summary of their choice and commitment (Romans 1:18-21, NLT): "But God shows his anger from heaven against all sinful, wicked people who push the truth away from themselves. For the truth about God is known to them instinctively. God has put this knowledge in their hearts. From the time the world was created, people have seen the earth and sky and all that God made. They can clearly see his invisible qualities - his eternal power and divine nature. So they have no excuse whatsoever for not knowing God. Yes, they knew God, but they wouldn't worship him as God or even give him thanks. And they began to think up foolish ideas of what God was like. The result was that their minds became dark and confused."

Sadly, those described in the above verses no longer sense or feel any shame for their behavior or lifestyle choices. With abandon, they have forfeited spiritual verities for a narcissistic and carnal life – answering to no one and pleasing only the flesh. They are an illustration of those whom the Psalmist describes in Psalm 14:1-3, "The fool says in his heart, There is no God. They are corrupt, they do abominable deeds, there is none who does good. The Lord looks down from heaven on the children of man, to see if there are any who understand, who seek after God. They have all turned aside; together they have become corrupt; there is none who does good, not even one..."

There is a similar statement given in the pericope (a selection from a book, especially a passage from the Bible) - Romans 3:10-23 – (selected), "...as it is written: None is righteous, no, not one; no one understands; no one seeks for God. All have turned aside; together they have become worthless; no one does good, not even one...Their mouth is full of curses and bitterness...and the way of peace they have not known. There is no fear of God before their eyes...for all have sinned and fall short of the glory of God..."

This is part of the result for the one who is bent on rejecting The Living God and the Gospel of the Lord Jesus Christ. This is similar to the behavior observed by God in Genesis 6:5-7, "The Lord saw that the wickedness of man was great in the earth, and that every intention of the thoughts of his heart was only evil continually. And the Lord was sorry that he had made man on the earth, and it grieved him to his heart. So the Lord said, I will blot out man whom I have created from the face of the land, man and animals and creeping things and birds of the heavens, for I am sorry that I have made them." This resulted in the Judgment of the Flood upon the earth. Only Noah – because he was a righteous man - was spared, along with his family. While the picture we have of God in the Bible emphasizes His love, mercy, grace and patience – His Word is clear that His Holy Name and Honor will be vindicated in His way and in His time. The question is not "if" God's judgment will come but "when" it will occur.

When man rejected God and the evidences of His being, Romans 1:24-32 continues and three times indicates that "God gave them up…" In this interval of time, the window of grace remains open and the message of the Gospel continues to be proclaimed and is operative for all who will believe.

(1) "Therefore God gave them up in the lusts of their hearts to impurity, to the dishonoring of their bodies among themselves, because they exchanged the truth about God for a lie and worshiped and served the creature rather than the Creator, who is blessed forever!"

(2) "For this reason God gave them up to dishonorable passions. For their women exchanged natural relations for those that are contrary to nature; and the men likewise gave up natural relations with women and were consumed with passion for one another, men committing shameless acts with men and receiving in themselves the due penalty for their error."

(3) "And since they did not see fit to acknowledge God, God gave them up to a debased mind to do what ought not to be done."

There is a list of the behaviors where those who reject the Gospel and righteousness seemingly devise every conceivable way and means to carry out sinful instincts and their deeds of unrighteousness without restraint or limit. Jesus reminded His followers in Matthew 24:37-39, "For as were the days of Noah, so will be the coming of the Son of Man…and they were unaware until the flood came and swept them all away, so will be the coming of the Son of Man." The scope of the sinful behavior is seen as Paul continues in Romans 1 - "They were filled with all manner of unrighteousness, evil, covetousness, malice. They are full of envy, murder, strife, deceit, maliciousness. They are gossips, slanderers, haters of God, insolent, haughty, boastful, inventors of evil, disobedient to parents, foolish, faithless, heartless, ruthless. Though they know God's decree that those who practice such things deserve to die, they not only do them but give approval to those who practice them."

There is no evidence of remorse or repentance. There is no regard for anything pertaining to God and His Word. Darkness is their choice and commitment. Their conscience has been seared and become desensitized to moral verities or righteous standards for life. They wallow in their sin and show contempt for anything righteous or holy. They have no fear of God before their eyes. They have no sense of any pending judgment for their sin and rebellion. They blind their eyes to truth and deafen their ears to the message of hope and deliverance. It is the truth of God recorded in the vision - Isaiah 6:9-10, "And he said, Go, and say to this people: Keep on hearing, but do not understand; keep on seeing, but do not perceive. Make the heart of this people dull, and their ears heavy, and blind their eyes; lest they see with their eyes, and hear with their ears, and understand with their hearts, and turn and be healed." It is both sad and heart-rending to know of those who refuse to seek the Lord while He may be found, and to call upon Him while He is near.

Personal Study Questions - - -

In the previous chapter, an Outline of The Roman Road – A Plan of Salvation was given. Have you ever used this or some other Gospel Presentation with anyone at any time? What kind of response was there?

If a person is difficult, rebellious, surly – should an effort be made to present the Gospel with such an individual? Does the fact that this person is a candidate to become a new creature in Christ motivate you to want to try?

If a person indicates they are not interested; they want you to leave them alone; they don't want you to approach them with the Gospel ever again – what should you do?

As you involve yourself in presenting the Gospel to those who are lost, including some who may be hostile toward God and that Gospel, may you be encouraged by the words of an old Hymn of consecration - - -

> Go, labor on: spend, and be spent,
> Thy joy to do the Father's will:
> It is the way the Master went;
> Should not the servant tread it still?
>
> Go, labor on while it is day:
> The world's dark night is hastening on;
> Speed, speed thy work, cast sloth away;
> It is not thus that souls are won.
>
> Toil on, faint not, keep watch and pray,
> Be wise the erring soul to win;
> Go forth into the world's highway,
> Compel the wanderer to come in.

Be strong in the Lord! Faint not! Be faithful in all situations! Do not be fearful! Let the joy of the Lord be your strength!

Great Delusion

The coming of the lawless one is by the activity of Satan with all power and false signs and wonders, and with all wicked deception for those who are perishing, because they refused to love the truth and so be saved. Therefore God sends them a strong delusion, so that they may believe what is false, in order that all may be condemned who did not believe the truth but had pleasure in unrighteousness.

II Thessalonians 2:9-12

The language is very pointed and strong regarding a day not too distant that will be marked by - False signs; Wicked deception; Refused to love the truth; Strong delusion; Condemned; and Pleasure in unrighteousness. A question lurking in the background of these verses and thoughts is: Why do people lie? Why is falsehood, deceit, misrepresentation, disinformation so imbedded in our culture and conversation? While the Scriptures are speaking of an end time lifestyle and practice, the secular world is also facing many of the same issues.

A few years ago (2006), Forbes Magazine featured an article entitled: "Most Common Resume Lies" by Kate DuBose Tomassi. "From foolish fibs to full-on fraud, lying on your résumé is one of the most common ways that people stretch the truth. But think twice before you ship off your next half-baked job application. Even if your moral compass doesn't keep you from deceit, the fact that human resources is on to the game should...The percentage of people who lie to potential employers is substantial, says Sunny Bates, CEO of New York-based executive recruitment firm... She estimates that 40% of all résumés aren't altogether above board...One of the most common résumé lies involves playing with dates to hide employment gaps. The reasons are myriad: hiding being fired, a period of job hopping or even an embarrassing prison stay. Some women stretch time lines because they fear it will be difficult to reenter the workplace after starting a family...Even though it's one of the easiest items on a résumé to check, bogus college degree claims are also prevalent...not having a diploma is one of the things many applicants are most ashamed about...Fear of ageism can lead to lies by omission. Older job seekers may fudge or leave off the year they received their degree, or lop off their early work history, to appear younger on paper...While it's easy to sympathize, it's also important to remember that the truth behind these lies will quickly become evident at the interview...Considering that a résumé is usually a single sheet of paper, there are surprisingly many opportunities for yarn-spinning. Recent college grads will raise their grade point averages or claim honors they didn't receive...And some people blur the line between familiarity and proficiency when it comes to technical expertise, such as knowledge of software programs..."

In a Public Forum, the question was asked and responses solicited in terms of Why People Lie? The general conclusion was: "Whether you're a judge, a caring wife, or a concerned parent, lying is one of the most common things done by individuals in society. Lying does not only take place within families, but between governments; businesses to customers; and others. Even though lying is generally thought of as a bad thing, can it be a good thing? Whatever the case, where does lying come from and why do we do it?

The four main reasons offered regarding why people lie are:

1. As a Joke - Many times individuals lie to tell jokes. Does that make it a good thing? Maybe not, but I guess it will depend on the person. If it is perhaps Halloween, and a group of kids are planning a scare, one of them might lie to get an individual trapped into their prank. Even in simple sarcastic conversations one may tell a lie, but was only being sarcastic with actually no intention of harming or deceiving the person. In either case, this form of lying, as a joke, is one of the reasons why people lie.

2. To Escape Punishment - Another reason why people lie is to escape punishment. If a child knows that he's done something wrong and is afraid he is going to get punished for it, the natural reaction of a human is to lie to prevent it. However, many times that just makes it worse, and so in some cases people know to tell the truth up front to avoid getting caught in a lie later. On the other hand, those that do tell a lie are simply doing so as a risk to avoid punishment.

3. Deceptive Gain - This form of lying is probably the most harmful. In many cases, it is no different than taking another's belongings or life, but many still seem to do it regardless of the outcome. Why do people do it? Well, that question can be debated. Many couples do this to cheat on their spouse. Many thieves do this to steal others' belongs. Many individuals do this to control the minds of people to get them to do what they want to do. Whatever the reason of this deceptive form of lying, most people do it as a form of deceptive gain.

4. **Confused Mind** - The final reason why people lie is when individuals don't know the truth. Perhaps the person is taught something, and it is passed on to the next. It may be a lie, but the person still believes it. So if they really believe it, then are they lying? They aren't lying intentionally, but are still doing so because of not telling the truth. With this form of lying, the reason why people do this is mainly because of blind believing, or fear. Many times (although unintentional) it can be just as problematic as to that which is done for deceptive gain.

The generalization and rationalization is that this is alright because "everyone" does it in one form or another. This kind of thinking allows for cruel and unfounded humor, such as, one can always tell when a politician is lying – if his lips are moving – he's lying! It's unfair and unfounded – but – it is the thinking of too many in these times in which we live. The culture has shattered the moral compass and the value system is buried amid the trash of the world. Let's return to the earlier questions: Why do people lie? Why is falsehood, deceit, misrepresentation, disinformation so imbedded in our culture and conversation? One other consideration is: When did lying begin? Who started it and why?

The Holy Scriptures provide us with an insight into the origin and subtlety of lying. deceit, etc. - Isaiah 14:12-14 - "How you are fallen from heaven, O Day Star, son of Dawn! How you are cut down to the ground, you who laid the nations low! You said in your heart, 'I will ascend to heaven; above the stars of God I will set my throne on high; I will sit on the mount of assembly in the far reaches of the north; I will ascend above the heights of the clouds; I will make myself like the Most

High." Lying began when the Day Star, the son of Dawn –
Lucifer lied to himself when he became convinced that he could
dethrone God. The Isaiah 14 passage states clearly what
happen. Lucifer said in his heart:

- I Will ascend above the stars of God
- I Will set my throne on high
- I Will sit on the mount of assemble
- I Will ascend above the heights of the clouds
- I Will make myself like the Most High.

Pride allowed him to deceive himself and to believe a lie of
his own making and choosing. As a result, he and one-third of
his angel-followers were cast out of heaven. Revelation 12:9
records: "And the great dragon was thrown down, that ancient
serpent, who is called the devil and Satan, the deceiver of the
whole world - he was thrown down to the earth, and his angels
were thrown down with him."

A second passage that speaks of the devil's ambition and
goal is seen following the Creation - Genesis 3:1-5 - "Now the
serpent was more crafty than any other beast of the field that
the Lord God had made. He said to the woman, Did God actually say, You shall not eat of any tree in the garden? And the
woman said to the serpent, We may eat of the fruit of the trees
in the garden, but God said, You shall not eat of the fruit of the
tree that is in the midst of the garden, neither shall you touch
it, lest you die. But the serpent said to the woman, You will not
surely die. For God knows that when you eat of it your eyes will
be opened, and you will be like God, knowing good and evil."
The devil is (a) contradicting the Most High God, and (b) deliberately lying to the woman. The subtle effort was to get the
woman to follow his own failed effort to be like God. The devil

knew that was impossible – he had already tried himself and failed.

However, in Genesis 3:5-8, the text states: "So when the woman saw that the tree was good for food, and that it was a delight to the eyes, and that the tree was to be desired to make one wise, she took of its fruit and ate, and she also gave some to her husband who was with her, and he ate. Then the eyes of both were opened, and they knew that they were naked. And they sewed fig leaves together and made themselves loin-cloths. And they heard the sound of the Lord God walking in the garden in the cool of the day, and the man and his wife hid themselves from the presence of the Lord God among the trees of the garden." What will Adam and Eve do now? They realize something is wrong and different? How can they deal with it? They made a horrendous choice. The singular act of believing the lie impacted the innocence of Adam and Eve and disrupted their fellowship and communion with God. Rather than the eager anticipation of walking and talking with the Most High God in the cool of the evening, they now hid from Him and tried their best to elude Him and escape from being in His presence.

A third passage demonstrates that the devil is relentless in his effort and seizes upon any opportunity to conquer God. This time he chooses to go after God's only-begotten Son. Matthew 4:1-11 records the devil's attempt and the stages of his effort: "Jesus was led up by the Spirit into the wilderness to be tempted by the devil. And after fasting forty days and forty nights, he was hungry. And the tempter came and said to him,

1. If you are the Son of God, command these stones to become loaves of bread.

But Jesus answered, It is written, Man shall not live by bread alone, but by every word that comes from the mouth of God.

2. Then the devil took him to the holy city and set him on the pinnacle of the temple and said to him, If you are the Son of God, throw yourself down, for it is written, He will command his angels concerning you, and On their hands they will bear you up, lest you strike your foot against a stone.

   Jesus said to him, Again it is written, You shall not put the Lord your God to the test.

3. Again, the devil took him to a very high mountain and showed him all the kingdoms of the world and their glory. And he said to him, All these I will give you, if you will fall down and worship me.

   Then Jesus said to him, Be gone, Satan! For it is written, You shall worship the Lord your God and him only shall you serve.

Then the devil left him, and behold, angels came and were ministering to him."

The Temptation of Jesus by the devil was in the same areas the devil uses when he tempts us today. We find the broad description of these areas in I John 2:15-17, "Do not love the world or the things in the world. If anyone loves the world, the love of the Father is not in him. For all that is in the world - the desires of the flesh and the desires of the eyes and pride in possessions - is not from the Father but is from the world. And the world is passing away along with its desires, but whoever does the will of God abides forever."

Temptation will usually occur in one of three places and/or ways:

1. The Lust of the Flesh
2. The Lust of the Eyes
3. The Boastful Pride of Life.

The devil is strategic as well as subtle. He knows one's area of weakness and one's vulnerabilities. Just because one may be successful in resisting the temptation once doesn't mean the devil will not re-wrap it and offer it at another time and in a different context. The devil is the enemy and destroyer of the souls of mankind..

A fourth passage is when Jesus was performing His miracles and declaring His Gospel, John 8:31-34 states: "Jesus said to the Jews who had believed in him, If you abide in my word, you are truly my disciples, and you will know the truth, and the truth will set you free. They answered him, We are offspring of Abraham and have never been enslaved to anyone. How is it that you say, You will become free? Jesus answered them, Truly, truly, I say to you, everyone who commits sin is a slave to sin."

While we rejoice with this message that the "truth will set you free", the Pharisees did not embrace that truth. Their discomfort with His words increased when He said – John 8:37-38, "I know that you are offspring of Abraham; yet you seek to kill me because my word finds no place in you. I speak of what I have seen with my Father, and you do what you have heard from your father." Jesus draws a distinction between the Heavenly Father and the father the Jews and Pharisees are following and serving. He is very clear in terms of what He means when He states – John 8:39-45, "They answered him, Abraham is our father. Jesus said to them, If you were Abraham's children, you would be doing the works Abraham did, but now you seek to kill me, a man who has told you the truth that I heard from God. This is not what Abraham did. You are doing the works your father did..." Jesus is clearly linking them to the devil and disavowing that they have any legitimate part and role among the Covenant People of God. The text continues - "They said to him, We were not born of sexual immorality. We have one Father--even God. Jesus said to them, If God were your Father, you would love me, for I came from God and I am here. I came not of my own accord, but he sent me. Why do you not understand what I say? It is because you cannot bear to hear my word. You are of your father the devil, and your will is to do your father's desires. He was a murderer from the beginning, and has nothing to do with the truth, because there is no truth in him. When he lies, he speaks out of his own character, for he is a liar and the father of lies. But because I tell the truth, you do not believe me."

Jesus raises the issue of Character with His detractors. If God were your Father – and – you had Godly Character:

1. You would love Me
2. You would hear My Word - I tell you the Truth.

However, Jesus goes on to clarify when He says, if you are of your father – the devil – you will exhibit his character:

1. he was a murderer from the beginning
2. he has nothing to do with the truth
3. there is no truth in him
4. he is a liar and the father of lies.

We ponder once again: Why do people lie? Why is falsehood, deceit, misrepresentation, disinformation so imbedded in our culture and conversation? When did lying begin? Who started it and why? The answer is clearly given and stated by

Jesus in John 8:44. Jesus says, if you are of your father – the devil – you will exhibit his character:
1. he was a murderer from the beginning
2. he has nothing to do with the truth
3. there is no truth in him
4. he is a liar and the father of lies.

John Newton wrote the Hymn in 1779, Though Troubles Assail Us. One of the stanzas contain these words:

> When Satan assails us to stop up our path,
> And courage all fails us, we triumph by faith.
> He cannot take from us, though oft he has tried,
> This heart-cheering promise, "The Lord will provide."

Personal Study Questions - - -

What areas do you find to be your most vulnerable or with the greatest weakness?

If or When you are being tempted, what are the first steps you should take to resist the temptation and the tempter?

What three things did Jesus do when the devil came to tempt Him?

Is there instruction and guidance for you in Psalm 1:1-3? Would it help to memorize it so it will readily come to mind when temptations come your way?

In 1890, Fanny Crosby wrote the words to Victory Through Grace. Be encouraged by these words:

Conquering now and still to conquer,
rideth a King in His might;
Leading the host of all the faithful
into the midst of the fight;
See them with courage advancing,
clad in their brilliant array,
Shouting the Name of their Leader,
hear them exultingly say:

Refrain
Not to the strong is the battle,
Not to the swift is the race,
Yet to the true and the faithful
Vict'ry is promised through grace.

Conquering now and still to conquer,
Jesus, Thou Ruler of all,
Thrones and their scepters all shall perish,
crowns and their splendor shall fall,
Yet shall the armies Thou leadest,
faithful and true to the last,
Find in Thy mansions eternal rest,
when their warfare is past.

May the Lord guard and protect your steps! Keep on looking
to Jesus always!

Great Distraction

Let no one deceive you in any way. For that day will not come, unless the rebellion comes first, and the man of lawlessness is revealed, the son of destruction, who opposes and exalts himself against every so-called god or object of worship, so that he takes his seat in the temple of God, proclaiming himself to be God. Do you not remember that when I was still with you I told you these things? And you know what is restraining him now so that he may be revealed in his time. For the mystery of lawlessness is already at work. Only he who now restrains it will do so until he is out of the way. And then the lawless one will be revealed, whom the Lord Jesus will kill with the breath of his mouth and bring to nothing by the appearance of his coming.

II Thessalonians 2:3-8 (ESV)

The Day is coming – when the attempt will be made to suppress Biblical Truth – removing in from the Culture and as a standard for the nation. Other things will be substituted and the effort made to supplant God's Word with lesser things. In case you haven't noticed, the Culture has already begun to embrace and practice lifestyle choices that are contrary to the Biblical Standard. It began with the removal of Bible Reading and Prayer in the school systems; allowed for abortion on demand; condoning and recognizing homosexual and lesbian behavior – now allowing for "marriage" between same-sex couples, and the adoption of children so a "family" can be established, etc.

The Church will hardly raise a whisper about such behavior, activity and lifestyle choices. The "message" of the "church" has been diminished and seems to want to conform to the social mores of the culture. Some Church Services can be attended and/or observed where the name of God is used in the most general way possible, and repentance for sin is usually not heard at all.

In the effort to find relevance in society and culture, a new theology emerged – Liberation Theology. The attempts to define it have been several. One that comes close to a realistic definition is produced by the Center for Socinian Studies. Their statement is: "Facing enormous problems in the society, some theologians realized that the traditional theology concerned with religious dogmas and abstract religious concepts lost any relevance. It became an abstract speculation removed from the original spirit of the Gospel message and out of touch with real life. On the social level it served the rich. They realized that if one really cared for and believed in the Christian ideals, one had to answer the question: 'How to be a Christian in a concrete historical situation?' The basic concerns in Latin America shifted thus from "whether one can believe what Christianity affirms to what relevance Christianity has in the struggle for a more just world." Out of such considerations was born "liberation theology," outlined for the first time by a Peruvian theologian Gustavo Gutierrez a few weeks before the Medellín conference. Gutierrez defined theology as a "critical reflection on praxis in the light of the word of God."

Liberation theology builds upon two basic principles: (a) it recognizes a need for liberation from any kind of oppression - political, economic, social, sexual, racial, religious; (b) it asserts that the theology must grow out of the basic Christian com-

44

munities and should not be imposed from above, that is, from the infallible source book or from the magisterium of an infallible Church. It explores the theological meaning of human activities:

1. It interprets Christian faith out of the suffering, struggle, and hope of the poor;
2. It critiques society and ideologies sustaining it, pretends not to lay down specific rules for how to struggle for justice, but stresses that a responsible commitment with class conflict is an expression of love for one's neighbor. Through solidarity with the poor theologians of liberation advocate the transcendence from class division to a new type of society;
3. It critiques the activity of the Church from the angle of the poor.

"The main theme, liberation, is considered at three levels of meaning which are interconnected.

(a) At the social and political level liberation is an expression of aspirations of the oppressed classes and peoples. This liberation emphasizes the conflict in the economical, social and political process between the oppressed and the oppressors.

(b) At the human level the liberation is conceived as a historical process in which people develop consciously their own destiny through the social changes.

(c) At the religious, salvific (redemptive power) level the liberation means liberation from sin, the ultimate source of all deviation from fraternity, of all injustice and oppression. It brings man back into communion with God and fellow men, which is the radical, total liberation.

These three processes cannot be separated, they form a unique, complex process ("proceso unico y complejo"). For the first time sin was formulated in social terms as a concrete social act and not in traditional way as an abstract, and even an allegoric personification in the person of Satan, or at best, a personal act. For the first time the religious, salvific plan was explicitly linked to the human experience in a society."

The "church" had tried Existentialism as a possible resolve for man's sense of eternity. It is defined as being: "A philosophy that emphasizes the uniqueness and isolation of the individual experience in a hostile or indifferent universe, regards human existence as unexplainable, and stresses freedom of choice and responsibility for the consequences of one's acts." That left mankind in the slough of hopelessness and despair – no certainty regarding eternity or what's out there after one dies.

The "church" also gave consideration to neo-orthodoxy. Ligonier Ministries gives this brief synopsis of neo-orthodoxy: "Karl Barth was the most important proponent of neo-orthodoxy during the first half of the twentieth century, and his work continues to influence the church today. Neo-orthodoxy was a reaction to the Protestant liberalism of the nineteenth century, which denied biblical supernaturalism and defined faith solely as a "feeling of absolute dependence." The bankruptcy of such views in light of the horrors of two world wars led Karl Barth and others to try to restore the Bible to prominence in the church. While neo-orthodox theologians take a step in the right direction, they do not go far enough. While neo-orthodoxy does not deny the supernatural character of the Bible, it does deny that its propositions are objective, inerrant truth. Its proponents redefine truth as an "encounter" or an "event." For the neo-orthodox, the Bible becomes the Word of God when the Holy Spirit uses the words of Scripture to bring us into an encounter with Christ. They say that the Bible as an objective source of propositions is never in and of itself God's revelation because God only reveals Himself in the events of redemptive history and in His interactions with us today."

The "church" seems to be always on a quest for something new and/or different. This has allowed for another influence within the "church", namely, Modernity or Post-Modernity. It is difficult to fined a uniform definition for what is being espoused. It does allow for the publication of many books but they either (a) repeat and quote from each other, or (b) retain a somewhat nebulous approach to the subject at hand. If one takes a cursory approach finding a definition for Modernity or Post-Modernity, he will find very sketchy material. The closest one might come to definition is the following introductory paragraph from InFed. In a release from a think-tank in England (InFed), the following statement is made about post-modernity: "So what is post-modernism?" Their answer is both surprising and appropriate – surprising because no precise definition can be uniformly given, and appropriate because a particular time-context will be the determinative response for a given period. InFed submits: "A major problem we have is trying to find a useful definition of post-modernism. Most definitions are hopelessly vague and often inconsistent with each other. There is a considerable amount of confusion about the terms: modernity, modernism, post-modernity and post-modernism. Modernism and post-modernism have tended to be associated with aesthetic and intellectual movements such as that in architecture and literature; modernity and post-modernity have tended to be used to refer to changes in social and economic institutions... However, this is not a hard and fast distinction. Much of the talk of post-modernism has been concerned with social and economic change." This sets one up in a "straw man" situation. The Post-Modernity group doesn't define what it believes or stands for; therefore, if one sets out to define the post-modernist, he can claim foul and accuse one of having built a "straw man" for an argument.

With the desire and quest to become more relevant, the "church" has allowed itself to become more irrelevant. In its hope to gain more communicants, it has produced what is lackluster and ignored. It has removed itself from what is foundational to that which is speculative. It has distanced itself from the splendor of the Gospel to that which is deemed to be the spectacular and with greater appeal. The result of all these various attempts at relevance has produced a weakened and emaciated "church" that is increasingly being ignored. I Corinthians 14:7-8 states, "If even lifeless instruments, such as the flute or the harp, do not give distinct notes, how will anyone know what is played? And if the bugle gives an indistinct sound, who will get ready for battle?"

A previous Chapter of this book – "Great Delusion" - began with these words taken from: II Thessalonians 2:9-12 (ESV)
"The coming of the lawless one is by the activity of Satan with all power and false signs and wonders, and with all wicked deception for those who are perishing, because they refused to love the truth and so be saved. Therefore God sends them a strong delusion, so that they may believe what is false, in order that all may be condemned who did not believe the truth but had pleasure in unrighteousness."

The language is very pointed and strong regarding a day not too distant that will be marked by - False signs; Wicked deception; Refused to love the truth; Strong delusion; Condemned; and Pleasure in unrighteousness. It seems as though the lawless one and his minions are making inroads and having great success. There are signs, miracles and other displays of power. People are getting used to it and are liking it. This must be right? Wrong!

Consider the words of Jesus in the Sermon on the Mount – Matthew 7:21-23, "Not everyone who says to me, 'Lord, Lord,' will enter the kingdom of heaven, but the one who does the will of my Father who is in heaven. On that day many will say to me, Lord, Lord, did we not prophesy in your name, and cast out demons in your name, and do many mighty works in your name? And then will I declare to them, I never knew you; depart from me, you workers of lawlessness."

These same words in The Message Paraphrase are striking and clear: "Knowing the correct password - saying Master, Master, for instance - isn't going to get you anywhere with me. What is required is serious obedience - doing what my Father wills. I can see it now - at the Final Judgment thousands strutting up to me and saying, Master, we preached the Message, we bashed the demons, our God-sponsored projects had everyone talking. And do you know what I am going to say? You missed the boat. All you did was use me to make yourselves important. You don't impress me one bit. You're out of here."

The New Living Translation phrases these same verses as: "Not all people who sound religious are really godly. They may refer to me as Lord, but they still won't enter the Kingdom of

Heaven. The decisive issue is whether they obey my Father in heaven. On judgment day many will tell me, Lord, Lord, we prophesied in your name and cast out demons in your name and performed many miracles in your name. But I will reply, I never knew you. Go away; the things you did were unauthorized."

One can only wonder about the "church" as it exists today. It is so easy to go through the motions of being a Church but miss knowing The One Who is the Head of the Church – Jesus Christ. It is so easy to write by-laws and statements of faith in terms of what a Church should be but miss out on following The One Who has called and said: "Follow Me, I will make you…" What He will make you to be will be in accordance with His will rather than the politics of the local church or a prominent person or persons who insist on it being their way or the highway. The "church" may receive much more rebuke from the Lord than any imagined or hoped for reward. The people who have joined the "church" and been coddled, but not corrected; who have been enabled, but not equipped – may well wonder and ask "Why?" the "church" failed to do its task and fulfill its responsibility to its members. Such a lament!

The Apostle Paul has an additional word in II Thessalonians 2:6-8, "And you know what is restraining him now so that he may be revealed in his time. For the mystery of lawlessness is already at work. Only he who now restrains it will do so until he is out of the way. And then the lawless one will be revealed, whom the Lord Jesus will kill with the breath of his mouth and bring to nothing by the appearance of his coming."

The Message Paraphrase states these verses: "You'll also remember that I told you the Anarchist is being held back until just the right time. That doesn't mean that the spirit of anarchy is not now at work. It is, secretly and underground. But the time will come when the Anarchist will no longer be held back, but will be let loose. But don't worry. The Master Jesus will be right on his heels and blow him away. The Master appears and - puff! - the Anarchist is out of there."

There have been different suggestions over the years in terms of Who or What the Antichrist is or will be. Some have speculated that he is a prominent religious leader – the Head of a large religious movement. Others speculate that it is some charismatic political leader who will appeal to peoples all around the world – and they will want him to head a one-world government. It may be that the Anarchist or Antichrist is already alive in the world and will suddenly emerge to be a dominant leader and force.

Jesus alluded to certain things that will occur in the future – some simultaneously – Matthew 24:3-14, "As he (Jesus) sat on the Mount of Olives, the disciples came to him privately, saying, Tell us, when will these things be, and what will be the sign of your coming and of the close of the age? And Jesus answered them, See that no one leads you astray. For many will come in my name, saying, I am the Christ, and they will lead many astray. And you will hear of wars and rumors of wars. See that you are not alarmed, for this must take place, but the end is not yet. For nation will rise against nation, and kingdom against kingdom, and there will be famines and earthquakes in various places. All these are but the beginning of the birth pains. Then they will deliver you up to tribulation and put you to death, and you will be hated by all nations for my name's sake. And then many will fall away and betray one another and hate one another. And many false prophets will arise and lead many astray. And because lawlessness will be increased, the love of many will grow cold. But the one who endures to the end will be saved. And this gospel of the kingdom will be proclaimed throughout the whole world as a testimony to all nations, and then the end will come."

While Jesus indicates the types of things that will take place, He reminds the disciples that they should maintain a singular focus, namely, "...this gospel of the kingdom will be proclaimed throughout the whole world as a testimony to all nations, and then the end will come." Focusing on other things are part of the Great Distraction. Our focus, commitment and energy must be in the spread of the Gospel of the Kingdom to the whole world.

Jesus shares another response to the concern of many in Matthew 24:36-44, "But concerning that day and hour no one knows, not even the angels of heaven, nor the Son, but the Father only. For as were the days of Noah, so will be the coming of the Son of Man. For as in those days before the flood they were eating and drinking, marrying and giving in marriage, until the day when Noah entered the ark, and they were unaware until the flood came and swept them all away, so will be the coming of the Son of Man...Therefore, stay awake, for you do not know on what day your Lord is coming...Therefore you also must be ready, for the Son of Man is coming at an hour you do not expect."

- Fact: You must be awake and ready!
- Why: The Lord is coming at an hour you do not expect.

The Missionary and Ministry Song by Margaret Clarkson and John Peterson is both moving and compelling - - -

So send I you to labor unrewarded
To serve unpaid, unloved, unsought, unknown
To bear rebuke, to suffer scorn and scoffing
So send I you to toil for Me alone

So send I you to leave your life's ambition
To die to dear desire, self-will resign
To labor long, and love where men revile you
So send I you to lose you life in Mine

So send I you to hearts made hard by hatred
To eyes made blind because they will not see
To spend, though it be blood to spend and spare not
So send I you to taste of Calvary

As the Father hath sent me, so send I you.

Personal Study Questions - - -

If you had to choose something in the "church" that is a distraction for you – what would it be? What can or should be done to correct it?

If you could redo or revamp anything in the "church", what would it be and how would you begin?

How would you move someone from a comfort zone to be engaged in the conflict for the souls of people?

May the Lord strengthen you so you will always be faithful!
The Lord will never fail you!
As an Evangelist said: Keep on keeping on!

Great Prevarications

You are of your father the devil, and your will is to do your father's desires. He was a murderer from the beginning, and has nothing to do with the truth, because there is no truth in him. When he lies, he speaks out of his own character, for he is a liar and the father of lies.
John 8:44

The Message translates John 8:44, "You're from your father, the Devil, and all you want to do is please him. He was a killer from the very start. He couldn't stand the truth because there wasn't a shred of truth in him. When the Liar speaks, he makes it up out of his lying nature and fills the world with lies." To be a liar, one who prevaricates means: "to speak falsely or misleadingly; deliberately misstate or create an incorrect impression; lie." The Online Etymology Dictionary states: "to prevaricate is - "to transgress; to make a sham; to deviate (that is, to walk crookedly). In Church Language, it means "to transgress" or "to speak evasively..."

Several years ago (2005), The University of Southern California conducted a study and issued a report on: Liars' Brains Wired Differently by Usha Sutliff. The study of pathological liars shows first evidence of structural differences in the area of the brain that enables most people to feel remorse. The study also found the first proof of structural brain abnormalities in people who habitually lie, cheat and manipulate others.

While previous research has shown that there is heightened activity in the prefrontal cortex – the area of the brain that enables most people to feel remorse or learn moral behavior when normal people lie, this is the first study to provide evidence of structural differences in that area among pathological liars.

The research – led by Yaling Yang and Adrian Raine, both of the USC College of Letters, Arts and Sciences – is published in the October 2010 issue of the British Journal of Psychiatry. The subjects were taken from a sample of 108 volunteers pulled from Los Angeles' temporary employment pool. A series of psychological tests and interviews placed 12 in the category of people who had a history of repeated lying (11 men, one woman); 16 who exhibited signs of antisocial personality disorder but not pathological lying (15 men, one woman); and 21 who were normal controls (15 men, six women). "We looked for things like inconsistencies in their stories about occupation, education, crimes and family background," said Raine, a psychology professor at USC and co-author of the study. "Pathological liars can't always tell truth from falsehood and contradict themselves in an interview. They are manipulative and they admit they prey on people. They are very brazen in terms of their manner, but very cool when talking about this." Aside from having histories of conning others or using aliases, the habitual liars also admitted to malingering, or telling falsehoods to obtain sickness benefits, Raine said.

After they were categorized, the researchers used Magnetic Resonance Imaging to explore structural brain differences between the groups. The liars had significantly more "white matter" and slightly less "gray matter" than those they were measured against, Raine said. Specifically, liars had a 25.7 percent increase in prefrontal white matter compared to the antisocial controls and a 22 percent increase compared to the normal controls. Liars had a 14.2 percent decrease in prefrontal gray matter compared to normal controls.

More white matter – the wiring in the brain – may provide liars with the tools necessary to master the complex art of deceit, Raine said. "Lying takes a lot of effort," he said. "It's almost mind reading. You have to be able to understand the mindset of the other person. You also have to suppress your emotions or regulate them because you don't want to appear nervous. There's quite a lot to do there. You've got to suppress the truth. Our argument is that the more networking there is in the prefrontal cortex, the more the person has an upper hand in lying. Their verbal skills are higher. They've almost got a natural advantage."

But in normal people, it's the gray matter – or the brain cells connected by the white matter – that helps keep the impulse to lie in check. Pathological liars have a surplus of white matter, the study found, and a deficit of gray matter. That means they have more tools to lie coupled with fewer moral restraints than normal people, Raine said. "They've got the equipment to lie, and they don't have the disinhibition that the rest of us have in telling the big whoppers," he said. "When people make moral decisions, they are relying on the prefrontal cortex. When people ask normal people to make moral decisions, we see activation in the front of the brain," he explained. "If these liars have a 14 percent reduction in gray matter, that means that they are less likely to care about moral issues or are less likely to be able to process moral issues. Having more gray matter would keep a check on these activities."

The researchers stopped short of asserting that these structural differences account for all lying. "This is one of the components," Raine said. "The findings need to be replicated and extended to other parts of the brain. What are the other neurobiological processes? We haven't had studies like this. It's exciting to us because it's a beginning study, but we need a lot more to flesh out this discovery."

Yang, the study's lead author, said the findings eventually could be used in making clinical diagnoses and may have applications in the criminal justice system and the business world. "If [the findings] can be replicated and extended, they may have long-term implications in a number of areas," said Yang, a doctoral student in the USC department of psychology's brain and cognitive science program. "For example, in the legal system they could potentially be used to help police work out which suspects are lying. In terms of clinical practice, they could help clinicians diagnose who is malingering – making up disability for financial gain. "And also in business, they could assist in pre-employment screening, working out which individuals may not be suitable for hiring. "But, right now, I have to emphasize that there are no direct practical applications," she said.

In their journal article, the authors mention that separate studies of autistic children – who typically have trouble lying – have showed the converse pattern of gray matter/white matter ratios. "The facts that autistic children have difficulty lying and also show reduced prefrontal white matter constitutes the opposite but complementary pattern of the results compared to adults with increased prefrontal white matter who find it easy to lie," the researchers wrote. "Although autism is a complex condition and cannot be taken as a model for lying, these results ... converge with current findings on adult liars in suggesting that the prefrontal cortex is centrally involved in the capacity to lie."

It's particularly perplexing when pathological liars infiltrate and gain some level of control in a local church. There can be devastating consequences when this occurs. Sadly, it may have as a root problem one of the basic principles of the Christian Faith and Practice. John touches upon this at the outset of his epistle – I John 1:5-10. Notice the areas and times when "lie" is mentioned. John writes: "This is the message we have heard from him and proclaim to you, that God is light, and in him is no darkness at all. If we say we have fellowship with him while we walk in darkness, we lie and do not practice the truth. But if we walk in the light, as he is in the light, we have fellowship with one another, and the blood of Jesus his Son cleanses us from all sin. If we say we have no sin, we deceive ourselves, and the truth is not in us. If we confess our sins, he is faithful and just to forgive us our sins and to cleanse us from all unrighteousness. If we say we have not sinned, we make him a liar, and his word is not in us."

The Message Paraphrase is very blunt: "This, in essence, is the message we heard from Christ and are passing on to you: God is light, pure light; there's not a trace of darkness in him. If we claim that we experience a shared life with him and continue to stumble around in the dark, we're obviously lying through our teeth - we're not living what we claim. But if we walk in the light, God himself being the light, we also experience a shared life with one another, as the sacrificed blood of Jesus, God's Son, purges all our sin. If we claim that we're free of sin, we're only fooling ourselves. A claim like that is errant nonsense. On the other hand, if we admit our sins - make a clean breast of them - he won't let us down; he'll be true to himself. He'll forgive our sins and purge us of all wrongdoing. If we claim that we've never sinned, we out-and-out contradict God - make a liar out of him. A claim like that only shows off our ignorance of God."

John doesn't mince any words – he is as clear and precise as one can be – nothing vague in his declarations - - -

1. "If we say we have fellowship with him while we walk in darkness, we lie and do not practice the truth."
   If one claims to be a child of the Light – Jesus Christ – but – avoids the things of The Light so one can enjoy the things of the darkness – John says: : we lie and do not practice the truth..."

2. "If we say we have no sin, we deceive ourselves, and the truth is not in us."
   The fact is that one should sin – less. However, in mak ing that a goal for one's life, the reality is the no one is sinless.
   Too often, a holier than thou person comes along and condemns those who do not live up to certain stan dards. Oftentimes, they make themselves the measure ing rod against which others are expected to measure themselves.

3. "If we say we have not sinned, we make him a liar, and his word is not in us."

4. The denial that one has sinned because it is saying God is wrong for believing that we al are sinning. John says it forthrightly – "we make him (God) a liar, and his word is not in us." This one would dare to make God the Liar. The reason why this occurs is that God's Word is not a part of that person's life. They may carry a Bible but seldom read it and rarely practice it.

The pathological liar-types are not just occupying pews in churches but are also in positions of leadership as well. One would only need to reflect on the dreadful behavior of pedophile priests and the hundreds of young lives that were affected and impacted by that behavior. Some of the reports that are easily accessible indicate: "In addition to cases of actual abuse, much of the scandal has focused around members of the church hierarchy who did not report abuse allegations to the civil authorities and who, in many cases, reassigned the offenders to other locations where the alleged predators continued to have contact with minors and had opportunities to continue to sexually abuse children... In the United States, churches have paid more than $2 billion in compensation to victims. In Ireland, reports Into clerical sexual abuse have rocked both the church hierarchy and the state. A nine-year government study, the Ryan Report, published in May 2009, revealed that beatings and humiliation by nuns and priests were common at institutions that held up to 30,000 children. The investigation found that Catholic priests and nuns for decades "terrorized thousands of boys and girls, while government inspectors failed to stop the abuse..."

Several members of the Clergy, and those elected to be Church Officers, or appointed as Sunday School Teachers have also neglected the maintenance of integrity in their lives and commitment. Many times they are allowed to continue because of who they are and because of what their family connections have been in the local Church. At this level of activity, many more become guilty by association of the lie being lived and practiced. It is a behavior that condones rather than condemns the wrong-doer. One needs only to read Revelation 2 and 3 and arrive at the conclusion that God does not condone evil and will not bless what He condemns. In many instances, Ichabod – the glory has departed – could be etched over the entrances of several particular churches. The person who would address the sin of living the lie would do so at his own peril. The locals will usually circle their wagons around the alleged offender and defend the erroneous behavior while attacking the one who is attempting to address the evil and error.

There are too many church-type people who allow themselves to become enablers. They make it possible and easy for the one who is living a lie to continue with that behavior. It was because of the enablers that we passed through some religious scandals. The PTL Club is but one example. Now – after years of incarceration and absence from the television scene, some enablers have developed a new site for the disgraced "minister" and Morningside near Branson, Missouri. Those who follow such spectacular events observed: "It's a stunning reversal of fortune for a man who fell so spectacularly in the late 1980s, when his $129 million-a-year religious empire crumbled; prison time and personal shame followed. A return to the airwaves seemed impossible. Yet no one here tries hiding the past. They acknowledge the striking similarities between Morningside and Heritage USA, a Christian theme park and resort in South Carolina that was the linchpin of the PTL empire. One man designed both, giving them the feel of dense European villages. Real estate, again, is part of the mission."

It wasn't restricted to the religious enablers. It also branched to the political as well. Who would soon forget a dominant political person looking into a television camera and declaring "I have not had sex with that woman…" Then as impeachment from office loomed, he once again was before a television camera and uttered the infamous words – "it all depends on what is – is…" Different supporters rallied to his defense and protested his innocence – even though they knew otherwise.

In a December 2010 devotional written by R.C. Sproul, he writes on the theme: "Putting Your Faith In Action." He goes on to state: "The organized church is torn with strife and distrust. Ultimately, the battle is not so much between conservatives and liberals, evangelicals and activists, or fundamentalists and modernists. The issue now is between belief and unbelief: Is Christianity true or false, real or unreal? What is deadly to the church is when the external forms of religion are maintained while their substance is discarded. This we call practical atheism. Practical atheism appears when we live as if there were no God. The externals continue, but man becomes the central thrust of devotion as the attention of religious concern shifts away from man's devotion to God to man's devotion to man, bypassing God. The 'ethic' of Christ continues in a superficial way, having been ripped from its supernatural, transcendent, and divine foundation...It is possible for the church to believe all the right things and do the wrong things. It is possible also to believe the wrong things and do the right things = but not for very long. We need right faith initiating right action. Honest faith—joined with honest action—bears witness to a real God and a real Christ..."

He continues with words of challenge: "Examine your heart today:
- Are you believing the right things, yet doing the wrong things?
- Are you believing the wrong things while still trying to do the right things?

Study - James 2:17-18: "Thus also faith by itself, if it does not have works, is dead. But someone will say, 'You have faith, and I have works.' Show me your faith without your works, and I will show you my faith by my works."

Also - James 2:26: "For as the body without the spirit is dead, so faith without works is dead also."

Personal Study Questions - - -

Have you had the experience of knowing about deception and/or immorality in the church you attend? What did you think should be done about it? What did you personally try to do about it?

If inappropriate behavior has occurred in your presence, did you know what needed to be done to confront such an offense? Did you take any action?

If an offending party is confronted regarding an offense and leaves the church that is trying to deal with the sin – and goes to another church – should that other church be informed?

What if they are made welcome in that other church, even though the sin is still active in the persons life, is there any recourse for the offended party or parties? Can it be overlooked because the other church needed a new member or members?

In a bygone day, children in Sunday School were taught a simple chorus that contains profound instruction.

O be careful little eyes what you see
O be careful little eyes what you see
There's a Father up above
And He's looking down in love
So, be careful little eyes what you see.

O be careful little ears what you hear
O be careful little ears what you hear
There's a Father up above
And He's looking down in love
So, be careful little ears what you hear.

O be careful little hands what you do
O be careful little hands what you do
There's a Father up above
And He's looking down in love
So, be careful little hands what you do.

O be careful little feet where you go
O be careful little feet where you go
There's a Father up above
And He's looking down in love
So, be careful little feet where you go.

O be careful little mouth what you say
O be careful little mouth what you say
There's a Father up above
And He's looking down in love
So, be careful little mouth what you say.

There's a great truth to be learned through these lyrics and to be implemented in our lives. A mental picture is "the great cloud of witnesses" surrounding us (Hebrews 12:1) either cheering us on when we do what is right, or remaining silent when we forget or ignore the words of the chorus above and err along life's path.

Great Possibility

Therefore the Lord waits to be gracious to you, and therefore he exalts himself to show mercy to you. For the Lord is a God of justice; blessed are all those who wait for him. For a people shall dwell in Zion, in Jerusalem; you shall weep no more. He will surely be gracious to you at the sound of your cry. As soon as he hears it, he answers you. And though the Lord give you the bread of adversity and the water of affliction, yet your Teacher will not hide himself anymore, but your eyes shall see your Teacher. And your ears shall hear a word behind you, saying, This is the way, walk in it, when you turn to the right or when you turn to the left.

Isaiah 30:18-21

Direction for a journey is best when it is clear and precise. There are times when a trip destination is programmed into a GPS (Global Positioning System) and the trip is undertaken. If one knows a better road and shorter possibility – and takes it – the GPS device will sound annoyed and displeased and issue a demand – "turn around." If one has chosen a workable route, the GPS will catch up and renew its directions from where one is in relationship to where one is going. Repeatedly, the Lord has issued directions for His people. The Decalogue (The Ten Commandments – Exodus 20 and Deuteronomy 5) is very specific in terms of what God requires and what performance of duty He expects. Similarly, when Jesus Christ taught the Beatitudes (Sermon on the Mount – Matthew 5), He was instructing in terms of a life of blessing and fulfillment as these truths for life were implemented. Neither the Decalogue nor the Beatitudes were issued as suggestions and/or options. They were/are meant as a revelation of God's direction for one's life. A life seeking to live in the presence of God will be frustrated and know failure if God's guidelines and requirements are ignored. A life desiring to realize the full extent of God's love, joy and peace will have to live one's life according to God's prescription for it. The words of Isaiah 30:18 – "Therefore the Lord waits to be gracious to you, and therefore he exalts himself to show mercy to you." - are descriptive of the Lord's desire to interact with His people and to have them benefit from His limitless grace and graciousness. This is Who He is and indicates the on-going relationship that can be normal for any child of God with Him.

To continue with the GPS concept, how is it that one can so easily become lost and be in a detour or dead-end situation? In Jeremiah 26:2-6, there is key and crucial element mentioned that will determine whether or not God's people will journey on the road of blessing, or find themselves on a detour leading to a dead-end. The Prophet spoke the message from the Lord: "Thus says the Lord: Stand in the court of the Lord's house, and speak to all the cities of Judah that come to worship in the house of the Lord all the words that I command you to speak to them; do not hold back a word. It may be they will listen, and every one turn from his evil way, that I may relent of the disaster that I intend to do to them because of their evil deeds. You shall say to them, 'Thus says the Lord: If you will not listen to me, to walk in my law that I have set before you, and to listen to the words of my servants the prophets whom I send to you urgently, though you have not listened, then I will make this house like Shiloh, and I will make this city a curse for all the nations of the earth."

This is an appeal flowing from the Lord Who longs to show and share His graciousness with His people. The key element in these verses is – "listen" – to the Lord and His Word. Rather than "listen", they confront God's prophet and threaten Jeremiah with death. The response of the priests, prophets and people is recorded in Jeremiah 26:7-8, "The priests and the prophets and all the people heard Jeremiah speaking these words in the house of the Lord. And when Jeremiah had finished speaking all that the Lord had commanded him to speak to all the people, then the priests and the prophets and all the people laid hold of him, saying, You shall die!"

The obvious is stated in verse 7: "The priests...prophets... all the people heard..." What is equally obvious is that they chose not to listen. Their response to Jeremiah – "You shall die!" - is a result of their disobedience, rebellion and rejection of the Lord. Their preference was to stay on the detour road that leads to a dead-end. They would rather be part of a blind-leading-the-blind group than yielding to the Lord of grace and graciousness. When the Scriptures state (Proverbs 14:8): "Fools mock at making amends for sin...", it speaks to those who choose the wrong road and way because of their personal stubbornness and rebellion. The Message translates that verse: "The stupid ridicule right and wrong, but a moral life is a favored life."

The issue for everyone who chooses stubbornness and rebellion is basically – if you won't follow the Lord, who or what will you follow? That's the basic issue raised by Joshua as he spoke with the people and challenged them in Joshua 24:15, "And if it is evil in your eyes to serve the Lord, choose this day whom you will serve, whether the gods your fathers served in the region beyond the River, or the gods of the Amorites in whose land you dwell. But as for me and my house, we will serve the Lord."

The choice is simple and plain – either The Lord or the various conglomeration of gods from a pagan culture. A television preacher made this observation about Jesus Christ, namely, He lived in a very small geographical location. Considering all of the land mass in the world, in a relative sense, Jesus lived in an area comparable to a postage stamp. This same idea is shared in the words written by Dr. James Allan Francis in 1926, One Solitary Life – Jesus has had more impact on history for good than any other person.

One Solitary Life gives the following as a summary of the life of Jesus Christ – "He was born in an obscure village; The child of a peasant woman; He grew up in another obscure village where he worked in a carpenter shop until he was thirty; He never wrote a book; He never held an office; He never went to college; He never visited a big city; He never travelled more than two hundred miles from the place where he was born; He did none of the things usually associated with greatness; He had no credentials but himself. He was only thirty three; His friends ran away; One of them denied him; He was turned over to his enemies and went through the mockery of a trial; He was nailed to a cross between two thieves; While dying, his executioners gambled for his clothing the only property he had on earth. When he was dead He was laid in a borrowed grave through the pity of a friend. Nineteen centuries have come and gone and today Jesus is the central figure of the human race; and the leader of mankind's progress. All the armies that have ever marched; All the navies that have ever sailed; All the parliaments that have ever sat; All the kings that ever reigned put together have not affected the life of mankind on earth as powerfully as that one solitary life."

In one of his writings, Josh McDowell made a historical point and asked: What did Napoleon say about Jesus? The answer given is: "I know men and I tell you that Jesus Christ is no mere man. Between him and every other person in the world there is no possible term of comparison. Alexander, Caesar, Charlemagne, and I founded empires. But on what did we rest the creations of our genius? Upon force. Jesus Christ founded His empire upon love; and at this hour millions of people would die for Him." He goes on to add: "Everything in Christ astonishes me. His spirit overawes me, and His will confounds me...I search in vain in history to find the similar to Jesus Christ, or anything that can approach the gospel."

Why is it that mankind chooses to miss the obvious? How can one justify or even rationalize that going the wrong way is preferable to the right way? If some secular leaders can acknowledge the uniqueness of Jesus Christ, why would those who were religious reject any consideration of Him and His Words? It defies common sense!

The thrust of Isaiah 30:18-21 is about the nature and person of God. Who is He? How does He interact with mankind? How well can He be known? How will an inter-personal relationship with Him work to the benefit of mankind? There are particulars that the Lord wants His people to remember. In Isaiah 30:18-21, He reveals the following about Himself - - -

1. The Lord waits to be gracious to you,
2. He exalts himself to show mercy to you.
3. The Lord is a God of justice
4. He will surely be gracious to you at the sound of your cry.

5. He responds: As soon as He hears...He answers you.
6. Your Teacher will not hide himself anymore
7. Your eyes shall see your Teacher.
8. And your ears shall hear a word behind you, saying, This is the way, walk in it, when you turn to the right or when you turn to the left."

In Luke 24, there is a beautiful picture of two men walking on a road to Emmaus. The description of these men is that they were sad and forlorn. They had decided to return home. All their joy and enthusiasm about Jesus had been drained from them when He was crucified and buried. A "stranger" comes alongside of them and they have no recognition of him. The conversation is neither ordinary or extra-ordinary at this point. It is two men conversing with a third who doesn't seem to know what has recently occurred in Jerusalem, As a matter of fact, that is precisely what they propose to him (Luke 24:18): "Are you the only visitor to Jerusalem who does not know the things that have happened there in these days?" These two men, who had been engaged in the ministry of Jesus Christ are now sorrowful and confused. Where do we go from here? What are we to do now that our Leader and Teacher has been killed? What would He want us to do? It has gotten to be late in the day and these two men are hospitable. They invite and insist that Jesus spend the night with them.

Something transformational is about to happen. As they dine together, the guest takes a loaf of bread – Luke 24:30-32, "When he was at table with them, he took the bread and blessed and broke it and gave it to them. And their eyes were opened, and they recognized him. And he vanished from their sight. They said to each other, Did not our hearts burn within us while he talked to us on the road, while he opened to us the

Scriptures?" They have this moment of reality – they see and comprehend that Jesus has risen from among the dead – and – He's alive. The disclosure to others will now take place. The two men who were on the road to Emmaus now have joy, hope, peace, joy – because Jesus, The One Who is the way, the truth and the life is alive and has decreed to generations: "This is the way, walk in it…"

Years ago, a Chorus became popular at Bible Conferences and then in Sunday Schools. It is called: My Lord Knows The Way.

> My Lord knows the way through the wilderness
> All I have to do is follow.
> My Lord knows the way through the wilderness
> All I have to do is follow.
> Strength for today, is mine all the way
> And all that I need for tomorrow.
> My Lord knows the way through the wilderness
> All I have to do is follow.

While the words have an obvious application for God's people coming out from Egypt on their journey to The Promised Lane; and while there is also an application for the men Jesus called out to be His disciples; in like manner, there is application for the two men on the road to Emmaus – and to us – as we continue on our pilgrim journey with the Lord. The message of The Lord is constant, namely, "This is the way, walk in it…"

Personal Study Questions - - -

In your pilgrim journey with the Lord and as you spend time in the Word, prayer and worship, are you always aware of how and when the Lord speaks to you? Is your spiritual ear attuned to hear His voice?

When you are absorbed in a situation and circumstance, do you wonder to yourself, or aloud, where is Jesus when I need Him the most? Is it possible that you are so focused on the situation or circumstance that you have missed the obvious?

If your Lord knows the way through the wilderness of life and all you have to do is follow, are you either tempted or prone to turn off your spiritual GPS because you know a better way and a convenient shortcut?

Many Churches and Christians think they know the best direction to go and seldom consult with God until long after the fact - is this wise to do? When Jesus said "seek first", what do you think He meant when he used the word "first"?

There are words to a devotional and consecration Hymn that are a reminder to heed the words of our Lord: "This is the way, walk in it..." It is most helpful when Hymns can be found that echo a Biblical text. It helps to underscore and emphasize the great truths being gleaned and learned from God's Word. One such Hymn is entitled: Wherever He Leads I'll Go - - -

"Take up thy cross and follow Me,"
I heard my Master say;
"I gave My life to ransom thee, Surrender your all today."
Wherever He leads I'll go, Wherever He leads I'll go,
I'll follow my Christ who loves me so,
Wherever He leads I'll go.

My heart, my life, my all I bring
To Christ who loves me so;
He is my Master, Lord, and King,
Wherever He leads I'll go.
Wherever He leads I'll go, Wherever He leads I'll go,
I'll follow my Christ who loves me so,
Wherever He leads I'll go.

Amen.

Great Walk

This is the message we have heard from him and proclaim to you, that God is light, and in him is no darkness at all. If we say we have fellowship with him while we walk in darkness, we lie and do not practice the truth. But if we walk in the light, as he is in the light, we have fellowship with one another, and the blood of Jesus his Son cleanses us from all sin.

I John 1:5-7

In a previous chapter, we noticed the word of the Lord to His people through the prophet Isaiah (30:21) – "And your ears shall hear a word behind you, saying, This is the way, walk in it..." The Christian walk is filled with potential and possibility. It is a process of growth, development and maturity. The process begins very much like the life of a baby begins, namely, needing to be fed and nurtured. Peter summarized it aptly when he said (I Peter 2:2-3), "Like newborn infants, long for the pure spiritual milk, that by it you may grow up into salvation - if indeed you have tasted that the Lord is good." When a baby is ready to eat, the infant will suck as quickly as possible until nourishment begins to flow into its body. Inherent in the words of Jesus as He taught in the Sermon on the Mount is this similar concept – Matthew 5:6 – "Blessed are those who hunger and thirst for righteousness, for they shall be satisfied." To hunger and thirst after until one is satisfied/filled, is the way in which one will be nourished and grow strong. The pattern of growth and health must be consistent and obvious. The baby cannot be allowed to suffer from malnutrition and fail to grow. In many third world countries, countless numbers of infants suffer from malnutrition. Their level of resistance to germs and disease are minimized. Sadly, it leads too often and too quickly to death.

The idea of Peter for the "newborn (spiritual) infants" is that they are properly nourished and cared for so they will become strong. The basic starting point is learning to read, memorize and meditate upon The Holy Scriptures. Psalm 119 states with complete confidence that The Word must be a prominent part of a person's life – the sooner, the better. He states it this way, verse 11: "I have stored up your word in my heart, that I might not sin against you." In verse 16: "I will delight in your statutes; I will not forget your word." And in verses 103-105: "How sweet are your words to my taste, sweeter than honey to my mouth! Through your precepts I get understanding; therefore I hate every false way. Your word is a lamp to my feet and a light to my path."

One would do well to begin as soon as possible to memorize portions from the word of God. Begin with the basics - one verse per week – keep reviewing it each day – and quickly in will become part of your heart and mind inventory. There are Scripture Memory Programs available through different organizations, most notably, The Navigators. There are others who have an organized memory program however, one has the capacity to locate certain passages and commit them to memory. A partial list could (or should) include - Psalm 1 and Psalm 23; John 3:16-17; I John 5:10-13; II Corinthians 5:14-21; Romans 8:28-39; Romans 10:9-10, 13. Elsewhere in this book is The Roman Road – A Plan Of Salvation (at the end of Chapter 2) containing numerous Scripture verses. One can also use these verses as an outline for memorizing the Word of God, as well as being prepared to give a reason to anyone who asks the basis of your hope of eternal life.

If memorizing is too difficult, at least read the passages frequently and become well-acquainted with them. Some hints for Bible Reading include – to get started – if you read five Psalms and one chapter of Proverbs every day, you will complete both of those books in a thirty-one day month. Another practical hint, begin with smaller books of the Bible. The Book of Philippians can be an excellent place to begin. The entire book of I John could also enhance Scriptural knowledge and memorization. Also, one could single out significant chapters for reading and reflection – such as: I Corinthians 13 - The Love Chapter; I Corinthians 15 - The Resurrection Chapter; Matthew 5-7 - The Sermon On The Mount; John 10 - The Good Shepherd; John 15 - The Vine and The Branches. One should be creative in selecting passages to memorize. It might include selection of topics – locating the "I Am…" passages in the Gospels; knowing the location of the Parables of the Lord Jesus; passages that demonstrate for us examples of outstanding men and women of God in The Old Testament; etc.

The Christian Walk - where one is nourished by the Word and growing strong - will also encounter different suggestions and recommendations in terms of how one is expected to live as a newborn Christian. As soon as possible, the one who has experienced a new birth in Christ will have to learn some basics for the Christian life. A starting point is to understand that one's chief end is to glorify God and enjoy Him forever. When one became a spiritually newborn child of God in the mid-twentieth century, many Churches and Groups would emphasize that the person must live in a certain way to model that he/she is edified and able to edify, as well as being one who will not cause another to stumble. It's a very great, and sometimes grave, experience. When one is instructed to attend and fellowship in a Bible believing, teaching and practicing Church –

which church should one choose. There is a large spectrum (a broad range of varied but related ideas or objects) from which one must choose. Does one select from the contemporary or the traditional; formal or informal; charismatic or non-charismatic; broad-based evangelical or theological and doctrinally based; a house church or a cathedral; etc.?

Years ago, some churches attached a list of what a "Christian" isn't supposed to do. There were five areas of "don't"!

- Don't smoke or use any tobacco products!
- Don't consume alcoholic beverages; don't buy or sell them; don't frequent establishments where it is served!
- Don't participate in any modern dance or go to places where it would pose a compromise for one!
- Don't play cards or be involved in situations where use of them involves gambling – Poker, Black Jack, etc.!
- Don't attend and/or view motion pictures!

If the "don't" areas were followed, that was an assurance that one had truly been saved and was growing in he Lord. There was also attachments to the "don't list" for girls who were trying to dress nicely, and who used makeup so their appearance would be positive. They were oftentimes deemed to be "worldly" because of their dress and/or appearance. The "don't" concept of Christianity produced a mischievous parody – " I don't dance, drink, smoke or chew – and – I won't go with the girls who do." In the pre-television day, many young people struggled with "guilt" and were afraid of being seen if they went to a Movie Theatre on a Saturday that featured a western, a serial film and numerous cartoons. One can only imagine how the "don't group" would legislate their views and judgments in the twenty-first century.

For years, the United States had Prohibition as a law of the land. There were organized groups that took a stand against the availability of beverage alcohol anywhere. The production of Moonshine and Bathtub Gin is not a myth or a film fable. A group that was founded in 1874, the WCTU – Women's Christian Temperance Union – was active in their opposition to the use of alcohol as a beverage inasmuch as they construed it to be a detriment to the family. An interesting entry in Wikipedia includes the following: "The purpose of the WCTU was to combat the influence of alcohol on families and society...They were inspired by the Greek writer Xenophon who defined temperance as 'moderation in all things healthful; total abstinence from all things harmful.' In other words, should something be good, it should not be indulged in to excess. Should something be bad for you, it should be avoided altogether; thus their attempts to rid their surroundings of what they saw (and still see) as the dangers of alcohol. The WCTU perceived alcoholism as a consequence of larger social problems rather than as a personal weakness or failing..."

In the latter part of the twentieth-century and into the twenty-first century, the pendulum has swung considerably in other and different directions. In many religious groups it appears to be an "anything goes" mentality. An avant garde – "a pushing of the boundaries of what is accepted as the norm or the status quo, primarily in the cultural realm" – tends to be the approach in many areas of the "Christian church" today. The issue has become one that deals with (a) one's liberty in the Lord Jesus Christ, and (b) whether or not a man, group or organization can exercise their prerogatives and bind another's conscience. An illustration that is useful here appears in a Chapter entitled "Matters of Conscience" in the book, A Puritan's Mind. It is the statement of Martin Luther as he stood before the Church Tribunal and was called upon to recant his Ninety-Five Theses. In his statement of defense, he said: "Since your most serene majesty and your high mightinesses require from me a clear, simple, and precise answer, I will give you one, and it is this: I cannot submit my faith either to the pope or to the councils, because it is clear as the day that they have frequently erred and contradicted each other. Unless therefore I am convinced by the testimony of Scripture, or by the clearest reasoning, - unless I am persuaded by means of the passages I have quoted, - and unless they thus render my conscience bound by the Word of God, I cannot and I will not retract, for it is unsafe for a Christian to speak against his conscience…Here I stand, I can do no other; may God help me! Amen!"

With things of this magnitude being shared, no one should become flippant in terms of his/her practices as a follower of Jesus Christ. There are expected behaviors for the child of God. There are certain scruples that should be embraced. To be very clear, a scruple is: "a moral or ethical consideration or standard that acts as a restraining force or inhibits certain actions." The child of God must have scruples and must exercise them.

From those who embrace either position, either strict separation, on the one hand, or complete freedom and liberty of conscience, on the other – both groups will supply Biblical citation for the view being embraced and espoused. It is truly regrettable when some choose to use Scripture as a "weapon" rather than as an instructive and edifying statement in terms of God's standard for righteous living and clarity in terms of His will. The following Scripture texts illustrate this thought. The first is found in II Corinthians 6:14-18 (New Living Translation). The thrust is that one must be a "separated" Christian – "come out from them…don't touch their filthy things…" The passage states: "Don't team up with those who are unbelievers. How can goodness be a partner with wickedness? How can light live with darkness? What harmony can there be between Christ and the Devil? How can a believer be a partner with an unbeliever? And what union can there be between God's temple and idols? For we are the temple of the living God. As God said: I will live in them and walk among them. I will be their God, and they will be my people. Therefore, come out from them and separate yourselves from them, says the Lord. Don't touch their filthy things, and I will welcome you. And I will be your Father, and you will be my sons and daughters, says the Lord Almighty."

This passage is often linked with I John 2:15-17 (New Living Translation), "Stop loving this evil world and all that it offers you, for when you love the world, you show that you do not have the love of the Father in you. For the world offers only the lust for physical pleasure, the lust for everything we see, and pride in our possessions. These are not from the Father. They are from this evil world. And this world is fading away, along with everything it craves. But if you do the will of God, you will live forever."

The second passage has as its thrust the need to keep one's conscience free and not bound by any man's regulations and/or Pharisaical scruple. It is found in Romans 14:1-12 (New King James Version – Excerpts), "Receive one who is weak in the faith, but not to disputes over doubtful things. For one believes he may eat all things, but he who is weak eats only vegetables. Let not him who eats despise him who does not eat, and let not him who does not eat judge him who eats; for God has received him...He who eats, eats to the Lord, for he gives God thanks; and he who does not eat, to the Lord he does not eat, and gives God thanks. For none of us lives to himself, and no one dies to himself. For if we live, we live to the Lord; and if we die, we die to the Lord...But why do you judge your brother? Or why do you show contempt for your brother? For we shall all stand before the judgment seat of Christ...So then each of us shall give account of himself to God."

Separation from worldliness is a subject that could easily occupy several chapters. Just by way of illustration, the first text is James 4:4. It is direct and states: "Do you not know that friendship with the world is enmity with God? Whoever therefore wants to be a friend of the world makes himself an enemy of God." The choice is clearly stated – Are you a friend of this world, or are you a friend of God? The second text has a two-pronged approach – Ephesians 4:25-32 – it is worldliness in terms of the flesh, or worldliness in terms of the spirit. The idea is shared very succinctly, that is, Worldliness In Terms of The Flesh - - - Verse 25: put away lying, Verse 26 put away anger...do not let the sun go down on your wrath, Verse 27: give no place to the devil. Verse 28: Let him who stole steal no longer. Verse 29: Let no corrupt word proceed out of your mouth.

The idea of Worldliness In Terms of The Spirit includes, Verse 20: do not grieve the Holy Spirit of God, by whom you were sealed for the day of redemption, Verse 31: Let all bitterness, wrath, anger, clamor, and evil speaking be put away from you, with all malice, Verse 32: be kind to one another, tenderhearted, forgiving one another, just as God in Christ forgave you.

The Christian Walk cannot allow for matter-of-factness or a getting-around-to-it syndrome. There is a promptness and discipline and diligence that must always be in place. It carries with it the import of "justice delayed is justice denied." A paraphrase could be "change delayed is change denied." The Christian Walk is not measured or determined by a list of what a Christian can "Do" and what separated Christians "Don't" do. It is all based upon one's relationship to the Lord Jesus Christ and what will please and honor Him. It is a transparent evaluation in terms of my will as compared to His will; my plans as compared with His plans; what I want to do as compared with what He wants me to do. One should never assume a posture of dictating the terms of a commitment made or a service performed. If He is the Lord and Master of my life, the servant should be ready to listen and do – not negotiate or barter. One must also guard against interpreting what God means or reinterpreting so His Word will conform to my schedule and convenience. Indelibly traced upon one's heart and mind should be the words of Colossians 2:6-7, "Therefore, as you received Christ Jesus the Lord, so walk in him, rooted and built up in him and established in the faith, just as you were taught, abounding in thanksgiving."

Personal Study Questions - - -

If you set out on the Christian walk, what is basic and fundamental as you begin your walk? Does Ephesians 6:15 give you a helpful hint?

What is vital and important as you plan and begin to walk? Does it have anything to do with direction, destination or length of the journey? Explain!

When the direction and destination has been determined, what is the greatest hindrance one encounters? (Think of your answer from a "worldliness" point of view!) Is it ever wise to divert one's attention from the journey's destination?

In terms of the Christian walk, Psalm 1 states three negative situations that would distract and cause one to detour. What are those three negative situations?

What is the implication in Psalm 1 of "walk not…?

What is the implication of Psalm 1 of "Stand not…"

What is the implication of Psalm 1 of "Sit not…"

In Psalm 1, is the warning given in terms of the possible progression that can occur if one compromises either one's value system or moral compass? Explain!

May the Lord enable to you to walk uprightly and sprightly – in all that you do and wherever you may go!

Great Character

For the love of Christ controls us, because we have concluded this: that one has died for all, therefore all have died; and he died for all, that those who live might no longer live for themselves but for him who for their sake died and was raised...Therefore, if anyone is in Christ, he is a new creation. The old has passed away; behold, the new has come.

II Corinthians 5:14-17 (ESV – Selected)

When new life in Christ begins, it means the new creation in Jesus Christ has occurred. From that moment forward, this new life means one no longer lives for himself, but for Him Who died for them and rose again. As this new life begins and develops, certain truths will be evidenced because of lifestyle choices and changes. The areas that will begin to be measured are: One's Competence; One's Character; One's Commitment; and One's Consistency.

In the secular society and culture, one reads and hears different comments about civil discourse. The obvious is that the society and culture needs to learn more about how to appreciate one another, as well as how to practice civility while speaking to or about one another. It is difficult to discover role models who can demonstrate what is vital to interpersonal relationships and day-to-day discourse. The most public people are either performers or politicians. There's a good chance that what one may hear all too frequently borders either on the profane or that which is purely partisan. Many times one could easily turn off the sound of news interviews and not miss anything at all – what is being said is both predictable and repetitious. It's easy to conclude that "talking-points" and "spin" are what the public will be subjected to in the present and foreseeable future.

A phrase that is often repeated while being often neglected is the impassioned thought shared by Martin Luther King, Jr. when he said: "I have a dream that my...children will one day live in a nation where they will not be judged by the color of their skin but by the content of their character." It is the phrase – "content of their character" – that has somehow been buried in the rubble of the current dialogue and diatribe. The term "racism" is thrown around in situations where it is unfounded and unnecessary. The "content of their character" has been blurred by political ambitions and compromises. It becomes more and more apparent – as our nation spirals downward toward bankruptcy – that part of the trend to bankruptcy is attributable to losing our way with regard to "the content of their character" as a requirement and standard for thought and interaction.

What exactly is "character"? The most definitive idea is: "the combination of traits and qualities distinguishing the individual nature of a person or thing." If one consults Dictionary.com, one will find there is a list of ten dictionary results and twenty-seven definitive statements regarding "character." We'll be content with the idea of "traits and qualities." A definition for "trait" is: "a distinguishing characteristic." Two of the more cherished traits in life should be (a) Integrity – one is committed to honesty in all aspects of life, and (b) Credibility – whether or not one is seen as being authentic, believable, dependable and uncompromising. Both Integrity and Credibility must be guarded and championed. No one should allow for any question to arise whether or not one is "real" and can be trusted implicitly (absolute and unreserved; unquestioning).

The Westminster Larger Catechism asks and answers regarding character and one's good name. The focus is on the ninth commandment, "You shall not bear false witness against your neighbor." The Larger Catechism expands the application of this commandment to the duties required – the obligation one has to fulfill before God in all relationships, namely – "...the preserving and promoting of truth between man and man, and the good name of our neighbor, as well as our own; appearing and standing for the truth; and from the heart, sincerely, freely, clearly, and fully, speaking the truth, and only the truth, in matters of judgment and justice, and in all other things whatsoever...and unwillingness to admit of an evil report... discouraging tale-bearers, flatterers, and slanderers; love and care of our own good name, and defending it when need requires...studying and practicing of whatsoever things are true, honest, lovely, and of good report." This is a solemn obligation and duty before God.

The definitive statements regarding Christian Character are several. One passage is II Peter 1:3-8, "His divine power has granted to us all things that pertain to life and godliness, through the knowledge of him who called us to his own glory and excellence, by which he has granted to us his precious and very great promises, so that through them you may become partakers of the divine nature, having escaped from the corruption that is in the world because of sinful desire. For this very reason, make every effort to supplement your faith with virtue... knowledge... self-control... steadfastness... godliness... brotherly affection...love. For if these qualities are yours and

are increasing, they keep you from being ineffective or unfruit-
ful in the knowledge of our Lord Jesus Christ."

The Message translates verse 8: "With these qualities active
and growing in your lives, no grass will grow under your feet,
no day will pass without its reward as you mature in your
experience of our Master Jesus." This is a starting point for
what will cause one's life to be seen as being real, effective,
and fruitful. It will set one apart as having authenticity, integrity and credibility. The content of one's character will begin to
gain in stature and maturity. One's life will begin to exude the
content of one's character in an unscripted way – free from the
emptiness and meaninglessness of words – while demonstrat-
ing the qualities that can only come from a relationship with
the Lord Jesus Christ. It's as though Jesus was saying to each
one – personally - Isaiah 30:21 - "This is the way, walk in it..."
What are the qualities and basics of Christian character? Peter
states that one should make every effort to supplement - -

- Faith: the person is trusting and believing God alone for
  salvation and all things.
- Virtue: the person has made a deliberate choice to con
  form his/her life and conduct to moral and ethical
  principles, and uprightness.
- Knowledge: the person desires to know Jesus Christ,
  and the power of His resurrection. It is an advance in
  terms of the nurture and admonition of the Lord.
- Self-Control: the person desires righteousness and godliness in and for life. Such a one maintains a personal
  discipline in terms of the moral and ethical values
  established by God.
- Steadfastness: the person is firm in purpose, resolution,
  and faith; unwavering and not given to compromise.

- **Godliness:** The person is conforming to the will and pur pose of God. Such a one desires God and hungers and thirsts after Him.
- **Brotherly Affection:** The person is devoted to others and honors them. It is the implementation of in humility considering others better than oneself.
- **Love:** The person is heeding John 13:34, "A new com mand I give you: Love one another. As I have loved you, so you must love one another.

There Is another helpful list of particulars and requirements for the development and growth in Christian Character found in the exhortation of Philippians 4:8-9, "Finally, brothers, whatever is true, whatever is honorable, whatever is just, whatever is pure, whatever is lovely, whatever is commendable, if there is any excellence, if there is anything worthy of praise, think about these things. What you have learned and received and heard and seen in me--practice these things, and the God of peace will be with you."

Some important and key words appear in verse 9: (1) learned, (2) received, (3) heard, (4) seen, (5) practice. These words are part of a basic discipleship principle, namely, it is more caught than taught. One being able to observe what is being taught makes it possible for the disciple to escape exposure to the dictum – don't do as I do, do as I say! The key words of verse 8 ratchet up the level of personal persuasion and fidelity. There is an emphasis on: "...if there is any excellence, if there is anything worthy of praise, think on these things: Whatever is true; Whatever is honorable; Whatever is just; Whatever is pure; Whatever is lovely; Whatever is commendable. This is the road and the pathway for excellence in the development of Christian character. These areas will require both vigilance and diligence so that they will be maintained adequately and in a way that will honor the Lord.

One reason for vigilance and diligence is the reality of the pressures and tensions that would try to influence and impact the area of character. It is a fact that one of the most persistent forces that causes some difficulty in the development and growth of Christian Character is the tension one faces in life's experiences. Paul shared a glimpse into one aspect of such tension in Romans 7:7-25. The Apostle Paul is instructing the Church in terms of the law and sin. In that instruction, he details the tension he encountered and allows that anyone is susceptible to that same tension in the new creation process. Just in summary form, Paul stated the gnawing personal problem with which he needed to cope: "So the law is holy, and the commandment is holy and righteous and good...For we know that the law is spiritual, but I am of the flesh, sold under sin. For I do not understand my own actions. For I do not do what I want, but I do the very thing I hate. Now if I do what I do not want, I agree with the law, that it is good. So now it is no longer I who do it, but sin that dwells within me...For I have the desire to do what is right, but not the ability to carry it out. For I do not do the good I want, but the evil I do not want is what I keep on doing...For I delight in the law of God, in my inner being, but I see in my members another law waging war against the law of my mind and making me captive to the law of sin that dwells in my members. Wretched man that I am! Who will deliver me from this body of death? Thanks be to God through Jesus Christ our Lord! So then, I myself serve the law of God with my mind, but with my flesh I serve the law of sin."

An apt definition and summary for tension is: "the state of being stretched or strained; mental or emotional strain; intense, suppressed suspense, anxiety, or excitement; a strained relationship between individuals, groups, nations..." In some instances, "tension" is both desired and acceptable. Something, or someone, must have the ability and desire to "stretch" without snapping. In human relationships, it is desirable to have those who are able to endure stress and tension without a result of snapping and breaking. Paul was able to manage the tension because he maintained a focus on his Source and Resource – The Lord Jesus Christ. After detailing his inner and persistent struggle, he asks and answers the crucial issue for all who are engaged in spiritual warfare – Romans 7:24-25, "Wretched man that I am! Who will deliver me from this body of death? Thanks be to God through Jesus Christ our Lord! So then, I myself serve the law of God with my mind, but with my flesh I serve the law of sin."

The paraphrase in The Message states, "I've tried everything and nothing helps. I'm at the end of my rope. Is there no one who can do anything for me? Isn't that the real question? The answer, thank God, is that Jesus Christ can and does. He acted to set things right in this life of contradictions where I want to serve God with all my heart and mind, but am pulled by the influence of sin to do something totally different."

Paul knew that he had been called by Jesus Christ into a leadership position as the Church was being established. He knew that in a leadership role and position, it is preferable to have one who maintain a tranquil spirit rather than one who displays erratic behavior. In any learning curve, the quest should be to find those with abilities and skills, as well as those who are striving after and living up to their potential.

When one is in College or Graduate School, grades are important. All are striving for excellence and acceptance. If one received a "C" for course work done, even if that was a passing grade in most situations, it was also an indication that one was not living up to his/her potential or expectation. A good and caring Advisor would (or should) encourage the student to work harder; research longer; and develop the skill to assimilate what one is learning and to have the ability to communicate what has been learned in a discernable and understandable way. This is foundational for anyone who aspires to make a contribution to the culture and society in which one resides and where one should have an impact. It is applicable also for those who will attain and assume Leadership positions. While a "C" is a get-by grade, it is not the grade with which one should become accustomed or content. However, when it come to Leadership, a "C" classification – in one sense - would be a mark of excellence. If one is to be a successful in Leadership, there must be a demonstrated attainment of nothing less than a "C" level. What is that "C" level? There should be, at a minimum, the following: (1) Competence – the person is able to do the task well and endeavors to improve skills and abilities; (2) Character – the possession of traits and qualities that allows one to model integrity and authenticity; the life is an example of the reality of both integrity and authenticity; (3) Commitment – one who is focused and who will carry out to completion the task that needs to be done; one who can be counted upon to be efficient and faithful in performance of duty; and (4) Consistency – one with predictable behavior and work ethic; a person free of peaks and valleys in personality issues and task performance. This is the mark of the Christian Life the way the Lord Jesus Christ wants it to be lived. This is the only way to be free of the voids and vacuums – marked by nothingness and emptiness - that so often occur in a well-intentioned but a lackluster life. The whole idea of being suspended or floating in nothing is sad and deplorable. One needs to avoid the voids and vacate the vacuums that can so easily occur.

The Book of Hebrews covers several important areas of/for life. There are Warnings as well as Calls to Commitment (one would do well to search out the "let us" commitment passages – start with Hebrews 10 and 12). In Hebrews 2:1-3 is the first of several warnings recorded in the entire book. This passage is addressing – The Danger Of Drifting. Note the words: "...we must pay much closer attention to what we have heard, lest we drift away from it. For since the message declared by angels proved to be reliable, and every transgression or disobedience received a just retribution, how shall we escape if we neglect such a great salvation?"

The picture is clear – drifting away from what we have heard and been called upon to be and do. One could think of a ship that has been loosed from its moorings during a storm and has become a vessel drifting aimlessly and precariously. The Sons of the Pioneers popularized the song of life from a cowboy's perspective in their song, Tumbling Tumbleweeds:

See them tumbling down,
Pledging their love to the ground,
Lonely but free I'll be found –
Drifting along with the tumbling tumbleweeds.
Cares of the past are behind,
Nowhere to go but I'll find,
Just where the trail will wind,
Drifting along with the tumbling tumbleweeds.

This is life being lived in the void and vacuum – aimless, directionless, purposeless, empty. Don't let that happen to you. Be diligent and a person of purpose. Set goals and – by God's Grace - achieve your potential. To this end, Hebrews 10 and 12 give words of challenge and encouragement with a series of "let us" goals for a purposeful and meaningful life. In Hebrews 10:22-25,

- let us draw near with a true heart in full assurance of faith, with our hearts sprinkled clean from an evil conscience and our bodies washed with pure water.
- let us hold fast the confession of our hope without wavering, for he who promised is faithful.
- let us consider how to stir up one another to love and good works,
- (let us) not neglect to meet together, as is the habit of some, but
- (let us) encourage one another, and all the more as you see the Day drawing near.

In Hebrews 12:1-2,

- let us also lay aside every weight, and sin which clings so closely, and
- let us run with endurance the race that is set before us,
- (let us) look to Jesus, the founder and perfecter of our faith, who for the joy that was set before him endured the cross, despising the shame, and is seated at the right hand of the throne of God.

No one should live a shabby Christian life. In Jesus Christ, we have all that we need for our completeness and effectiveness. We have these words of assurance in Colossians 2:9-10 (NKJV), "For in Him (Christ) dwells all the fullness of the Godhead bodily; and you are complete in Him, who is the head of all principality and power."

This can and should be the way in which your Christian Life is being lived. Even when there are moments where you may falter, don't give up – just get up - and continue on with your walk in the Lord, and continue to grow in your knowledge of His will for your life.

Personal Study Questions - - -

Have you ever conducted a review and inventory of you character traits and qualities? How long ago has it been?

What do you think Peter meant and intended when he wrote in II Peter 1:8 (ESV) – "For if these qualities are yours and are increasing, they keep you from being ineffective or unfruit-ful in the knowledge of our Lord Jesus Christ."?

Peter lists 8 qualities in II Peter 1 that all should possess and where they should be increasing? Are there areas here where you could and should improve?

The Christian Life and Character should never be allowed to become stagnant or dormant. Has atrophy occurred in any of these character qualities in your life? If so, what do you intend to do about it? When will you begin?

May the Lord keep you focused and faithful!

Great Shepherd

Have this mind among yourselves, which is yours in Christ Jesus, who, though he was in the form of God, did not count equality with God a thing to be grasped, but made himself nothing, taking the form of a servant, being born in the likeness of men. And being found in human form, he humbled himself by becoming obedient to the point of death, even death on a cross. Therefore God has highly exalted him and bestowed on him the name that is above every name, so that at the name of Jesus every knee should bow, in heaven and on earth and under the earth, and every tongue confess that Jesus Christ is Lord, to the glory of God the Father.

Philippians 2:5-11

If discipleship means to follow the simple learning process, namely, "it's more caught than taught", the questions are: From whom is it caught? and What does one have to do to catch it? One would be wise to seek out an example or examples that can serve as a model that can be followed. The wisest choice one can make is to follow Jesus Christ and His teaching. When Jesus began to call men to be His disciples, He said to them (Matthew 4:18-22), "Follow me, and I will make you fishers of men." The key to their learning was their readiness and willingness to follow Jesus. What does follow mean? There are several definitions given, but for our study, we will use just a few of them. Follow means: "to go or come after in the same direction... to come after as a logical or natural consequence... to watch closely or continuously... to help in the cause of or accept the leadership of..." In the above passage, when Jesus said – "Follow Me!" – Peter, Andrew, James and John – stopped what they were doing and immediately responded and followed Jesus.

There's an interesting secular song that was popularized several years ago by Tom Jones that contained this lyric - - -

> Try to remember the kind of September
> When life was slow and oh, so mellow.
> Try to remember the kind of September
> When grass was green and grain was yellow.
> Try to remember the kind of September
> When you were a tender and callow fellow,
> Try to remember and if you remember then follow.

Each stanza closes with the same words: "Try to remember and if you remember then follow...follow...follow."

Several years previous to the secular song, there was a simple and direct spiritual song that encouraged many in their pursuit of God's will for their life. The song contained some of the following words...

> I have decided to follow Jesus...
> No turning back, no turning back...

> Though none will join me, still I will follow,,,
> No turning back, no turning back.

> The cross before me, the world behind me...
> No turning back, no turning back...

There were many scenes and occasions in the ministry of Jesus Christ where he focused on the cost of discipleship. One of these moments was in Matthew 8:18-23, "Now when Jesus saw a crowd around him, he gave orders to go over to the other side. And a scribe came up and said to him, Teacher, I will follow you wherever you go. And Jesus said to him, Foxes have holes, and birds of the air have nests, but the Son of Man has nowhere to lay his head. Another of the disciples said to him, Lord, let me first go and bury my father. And Jesus said to him, Follow me, and leave the dead to bury their own dead. And when he got into the boat, his disciples followed him."

Jesus is stating a basic principle in and for discipleship, namely, following Jesus must be the first and only priority in one's life. If one tries to excuse himself from the priority for even a seemingly important reason – Jesus is very direct when He says – you cannot be My disciple if you equate secular matters with spiritual commitment. The Scribe in verse 18 may have been very sincere and compelled by emotion and inclination. Jesus wanted him to know that comforts and luxuries were not a common or promised part of being a disciple. Jesus also wants to acquaint the disciples with the concept of the cross. Jesus knows why He has come and what He will suffer in just a few months. If the disciples are to follow Him effectively, they must deal with and find an identity with the cross. Jesus states this in just a few words in Matthew 16:24-27, "Then Jesus told his disciples, If anyone would come after me, let him deny himself and take up his cross and follow me. For whoever would save his life will lose it, but whoever loses his life for my sake will find it. For what will it profit a man if he gains the whole world and forfeits his soul? Or what shall a man give in return for his soul?"

When Luke records this moment, he inserts the word "daily" – so the text reads: "...let him deny himself and take up his cross daily and follow Me…" Luke is underscoring the importance of identity with the cross – it is a constant and daily identification – not an occasional mood-swing or moment of recommitment… The emphasis needs to be on the daily exercise and practice of being identified with Jesus Christ and His cross – totally and unequivocally. So many people wear a cross as jewelry and find their way to a church on Ash Wednesday, Palm Sunday, Maundy Thursday or Good Friday, Easter – for the brief annual celebration of the Death, Burial and Resurrection of Jesus Christ. Somewhere in the human rationale, one may mystically and/or magically equate a season of observation with "take up his cross daily and follow Me." It is a convenient way to dismiss the daily discipline of following Christ. In actuality, it is viewing the life and sacrifice of Christ – the Cross – with a passive shrug and indifference.

When Jesus is met by a young rich man who asks: "What good deed must I do to have eternal life?" – Jesus uses this encounter as a teaching moment for His disciples. In Matthew 19:24-30, there is an application made and an interaction by the disciples. "Again I tell you, it is easier for a camel to go through the eye of a needle than for a rich person to enter the kingdom of God. When the disciples heard this, they were greatly astonished, saying, Who then can be saved? But Jesus looked at them and said, With man this is impossible, but with God all things are possible. Then Peter said in reply, See, we have left everything and followed you. What then will we have? Jesus said to them, Truly, I say to you, in the new world, when the Son of Man will sit on his glorious throne, you who have followed me will also sit on twelve thrones, judging the twelve tribes of Israel. And everyone who has left houses or brothers or sisters or father or mother or children or lands, for my name's sake, will receive a hundredfold and will inherit eternal life. But many who are first will be last, and the last first."

The intriguing comment and exchange appears in the words of the disciples and Jesus' response to them. The disciples say and ask: "See, we have left everything and followed you. What then will we have?" It seems as though they are thinking in terms of the temporal and material, perhaps even the carnal. What then will we have? What's in it for me? What kind of annuity or pension will I receive? Jesus directs their attention from the temporal to the eternal when He says: "I say to you, in the new world, when the Son of Man will sit on his glorious throne, you who have followed me will also sit on twelve thrones, judging the twelve tribes of Israel. And everyone who has left houses or brothers or sisters or father or mother or children or lands, for my name's sake, will receive a hundred-fold and will inherit eternal life..."

Within our culture, we have tended to drift away from "eternity's values" and become absorbed with immediate self-gratification. As a result, we find our concerns in the temporal – what's in it for me now? – rather than the eternal – "How best will this advance and enhance the kingdom of God?" We have a clear and precise statement in terms of the kingdom of God and what will advance and enhance it. In John 6:37-40, Jesus said: "All that the Father gives me will come to me, and whoever comes to me I will never cast out. For I have come down from heaven, not to do my own will but the will of him who sent me. And this is the will of him who sent me, that I should lose nothing of all that he has given me, but raise it up on the last day. For this is the will of my Father, that everyone who looks on the Son and believes in him should have eternal life, and I will raise him up on the last day."

If Jesus came "not to do my own will but the will of him who sent me", what should that mean and require of each one of His followers? Should our level of commitment be any less than His? Should our focus differ from His? What task should demand one's effort and energy? Is there any excuse that could be offered to relieve one of that duty, opportunity and privilege? If one is not doing what the Master is doing, is that one following or being a maverick?

The words of John 10:27-30 are so tender on the one hand and compelling on the other. Jesus is declaring and clarifying His Mission and Ministry. He says: "My sheep hear my voice, and I know them, and they follow me. I give them eternal life, and they will never perish, and no one will snatch them out of my hand. My Father, who has given them to me, is greater than all, and no one is able to snatch them out of the Father's hand. I and the Father are one."

Jesus calls to His sheep. The sheep hear and recognize His voice. He knows His sheep. The response of the sheep – they follow Him. The Shepherd has the authority to give to the sheep eternal life, and the assurance that they will never perish. No one can snatch the sheep out of the Shepherd's hand. There is a certain criteria for the sheep who follows, John 10:5 - "A stranger they will not follow, but they will flee from him, for they do not know the voice of strangers." The sheep have learned to differentiate between the voice of The Shepherd and the voice of the stranger. In other words, they know who to follow and who to avoid following. They are attuned to The Shepherd's voice, words and directives.

In John 12:26, Jesus emphasizes – "If anyone serves me, he must follow me; and where I am, there will my servant be also. If anyone serves me, the Father will honor him." The sheep have developed and learned one skill and task, namely, to hear and heed the Shepherd's voice and to go along the path's of righteousness selected by The Shepherd. Only The Shepherd knows the best and right way for the sheep. All the sheep need to do is follow The Shepherd – wherever He leads the sheep follow.

In John 21:19-22, there is a succinct summary regarding what Jesus wants His disciples to do. These verses appear after Peter has given his threefold confession that he really does love Jesus, and heard Jesus commission him to feed His sheep and lambs. Then verse 19-22 appear: "(This he said to show by what kind of death he was to glorify God.) And after saying this he said to him, Follow me. Peter turned and saw the disciple whom Jesus loved following them, the one who had been reclining at table close to him and had said, Lord, who is it that is going to betray you? When Peter saw him, he said to Jesus, Lord, what about this man? Jesus said to him, If it is my will that he remain until I come, what is that to you? You follow me!"

Jesus is reinforcing for Peter and all the other disciples that their concern should not be details regarding the "who" and "why" but solely on their faithfully and consistently following Him. The sheep need to recognize and know His voice. The sheep need to trust and unhesitatingly follow Him. The sheep need to demonstrate their confidence in the Shepherd – He knows the best and safest path; He knows where the verdant pastures are located; He knows where the most calm and cool streams of refreshing water can be found. All the sheep need to do is to follow the Shepherd and stay close to His side.

Personal Study Questions - - -

What do you personally think it means "to follow"?

Have you ever been part of a caravan where everyone was supposed to follow the lead car – but you felt it was going too slow – so you passed everyone and arrived at the destination earlier than the others? What do you think this indicates about you?

When it comes to an following, are you willing to accept any task and duplicate that ministry even if it is less than desirable and is unpleasant?

What is the best way to have others follow you? Can you command or demand that others follow you? Why?

During major wars, where were the most effective Generals – with the troops on the frontline or in a command post miles away from the primary battle?

In Spiritual Warfare, where do you think Jesus wants you to be? In Ephesians 6 – The Whole Armor of God – why are we told to put it on? Explain your answer.

Be strong in the Lord and in the strength of His might!

Great Example

The Lord is my shepherd; I have everything I need. He lets me rest in green meadows; He leads me beside peaceful streams. He renews my strength. He guides me along right paths, bringing honor to his name. Even when I walk through the dark valley of death, I will not be afraid, for You are close beside me.
Psalm 23:1-4 (New Living Translation)

Jesus details a very important and critical area for the sheep who are called to follow Him. The detail is found in John 13:12-17 where Jesus has been washing the disciples' feet. Jesus is sharing basic and important truths with His disciples and then states - "When he had washed their feet and put on his outer garments and resumed his place, he said to them, Do you understand what I have done to you? You call me Teacher and Lord, and you are right, for so I am. If I then, your Lord and Teacher, have washed your feet, you also ought to wash one another's feet. For I have given you an example, that you also should do just as I have done to you. Truly, truly, I say to you, a servant is not greater than his master, nor is a messenger greater than the one who sent him. If you know these things, blessed are you if you do them."

This is the key instruction – "For I have given you an example, that you also should do just as I have done to you." He goes on to say, "If you know these things, blessed are you if you do them." These are the terms – example, know, do – if the example is followed and words are translated into action, it will result in blessing in one's life. If they are ignored, it will result in defeat and loss. Some questions worth pondering are: (1)

How many close and reliable friends do you have? (2) How many great people of reputation do you know? (3) How many people are outstanding examples that you can safely follow? (4) How many other people are following these friends and acquaintances you know and have? (5) What does it take to make you want to quit in terms of (a) seeking a worthy example for others to follow, or (b) being chosen as an example when you know there are negative things in your life that could be harmful and/or detrimental in another's life?

There are several examples that illustrate for us courage, sacrifice, faith, confidence – men who had become fully persuaded that God plus one is a majority. While there are several that could be selected, the first pair are Joshua and Caleb. They were part of the leadership of the tribes that were sent by Moses into the Promised Land to bring back a report about the land and any challenges that they would possibly encounter. Twelve men scouted out the land and returned back with their report. The report is given in Numbers 13 and 14. Ten of the spies return after forty days with a negative report. Numbers 13: "We are not able to go up against the people, for they are stronger than we are. So they brought to the people of Israel a bad report of the land that they had spied out, saying, The land, through which we have gone to spy it out, is a land that devours its inhabitants, and all the people that we saw in it are of great height. And there we saw the Nephilim...and we seemed to ourselves like grasshoppers, and so we seemed to them."

The two errors in the judgment of the ten spies was (a) they failed to reckon that the battle is not theirs but the Lord's, and (b) they allowed themselves to think they were small and incapable like grasshoppers. In both instances, they had surrender their faith and confidence in God and what He would do in their behalf. Also, they were too willing to shout down Caleb and Joshua with their alternative view. Their view is given in Numbers 14:6-9, "And Joshua the son of Nun and Caleb...who were among those who had spied out the land, tore their clothes and said to all the congregation of the people of Israel, The land, which we passed through to spy it out, is an exceedingly good land. If the Lord delights in us, he will bring us into this land and give it to us, a land that flows with milk and honey. Only do not rebel against the Lord. And do not fear the people of the land, for they are bread for us. Their protection is removed from them, and the Lord is with us; do not fear them."

They urge the people not to rebel against the Lord. They also urge the people not to fear the people of the land. They boldly state- "Their protection is removed from them, and the Lord is with us, do not fear them. The response of the people is less than charitable. Their design is to stone Joshua and Caleb – but – the Glory of God appeared to all the people. Moses intercedes in behalf of the people – Numbers 14:17-19 – "And now, please let the power of the Lord be great as you have promised, saying, The Lord is slow to anger and abounding in steadfast love, forgiving iniquity and transgression, but he will by no means clear the guilty, visiting the iniquity of the fathers on the children, to the third and the fourth generation. Please pardon the iniquity of this people, according to the greatness of your steadfast love, just as you have forgiven this people, from Egypt until now."

What could have been gained and enjoyed immediately would now require forty-years of delay until the rebellious generation died in the wilderness. So often, this is the case of people who lack faith and confidence in God. They are part of a group with limited vision - an overwhelming majority of people failing to comprehend the consequences for their lack of faith, their willfulness and rebellion. They missed out on all that God wanted to do for them and would allow them to enjoy. Only Joshua and Caleb would realize all of the beauty and benefit of The Promised Land. They alone would grow stronger in the Lord, as well as the increase of faith and confidence in Him.

The second example that illustrates for us courage, sacrifice, faith and confidence is Elijah and his servant. I Kings 18 shows the power of God in the midst of Ahab and the prophets of Baal. The crucial part of this event is whether or not the people will return to the Lord and take their stand for Him in the midst of a pagan culture. In I Kings 18:21, Elijah challenges the people forthrightly when he said: "...How long will you go limping between two different opinions? If the Lord is God, follow him; but if Baal, then follow him. And the people did not answer him a word." A great moment and opportunity but the people remained silent and refused to identify themselves with the Lord and His prophet Elijah. The prophet and his servant are undaunted. There is a crucial test that must take place, namely, will it rain at the word of the Prophet! I kings 18:41-48 shares the details of this faith and confidence adventure – "And Elijah said to Ahab, Go up, eat and drink, for there is a sound of the rushing of rain. So Ahab went up to eat and to drink. And Elijah went up to the top of Mount Carmel. And he bowed himself down on the earth and put his face between his knees. And he said to his servant, Go up now, look toward the sea. And he went up and looked and said, There is nothing. And he said, Go again, seven times. And at the seventh time he said, Behold, a little cloud like a man's hand is rising from the sea. And he said, Go up, say to Ahab, Prepare your chariot and go down, lest the rain stop you. And in a little while the heavens grew black with clouds and wind, and there was a great rain. And Ahab rode and went to Jezreel. And the hand of the Lord was on Elijah, and he gathered up his garment and ran before Ahab to the entrance of Jezreel."

Elijah had declared to Ahab "...there is a sound of the rushing of rain..." However, there was nothing in the heavens to indicate that – not even a cloud. Elijah tells and urges his servant to keep looking. Finally, the seventh time, the servant returns saying: "Behold, a little cloud like a man's hand is rising from the sea..." That's all Elijah needs! He tells his servant to go to Ahab and tell him to get into his chariot and get off of the mountain before the deluge of rain makes the roads impassable. It reinforces the saying that "little is much when God is in it." It also underscores the words of Jesus to His disciples in terms of the amount of faith necessary to accomplish exploits for the Lord. In Matthew 17:18-21, "And Jesus rebuked the demon, and it came out of him, and the boy was healed instantly. Then the disciples came to Jesus privately and said, Why could we not cast it out? He said to them, Because of your little faith. For truly, I say to you, if you have faith like a grain of mustard seed, you will say to this mountain, Move from here to there, and it will move, and nothing will be impossible for you."

The phrase that should leap out to you is "...nothing will be impossible for you." If you have faith and confidence that a cloud the size of a man's hand is the sign of a deluge of rain, and if the tiniest seed – one grain of the mustard seed – is adequate to the casting out of demons – why is it most people exhibit so little faith? Why is it we become reluctant to believe the impossible is possible by God's power? Hopefully, these illustrations and examples of faith will encourage and embolden each of us to have more faith in our God. Sometimes, we are like the people on Mount Carmel – silent – saying not a word, not a sound - rather than bold and confident in the Lord! We should always be reminded of the words written by Paul in Ephesians 3:20-21 (ESV), "Now to him who is able to do far more abundantly than all that we ask or think, according to the power at work within us, to him be glory in the church and in Christ Jesus throughout all generations, forever and ever. Amen."

A third example is Daniel and his three friends after they have been taken captive and moved into Babylon. A brief historical background is given in Daniel 1:1-7 (New Living Translation), "During the third year of King Jehoiakim's reign in Judah, King Nebuchadnezzar of Babylon came to Jerusalem and besieged it with his armies...When Nebuchadnezzar returned to Babylon, he took with him some of the sacred objects from the Temple of God and placed them in the treasure-house of his god in the land of Babylonia. Then the king ordered Ashpenaz, who was in charge of the palace officials, to bring to the palace some of the young men of Judah's royal family and other noble families...Select only strong, healthy, and good-looking young men...Make sure they are well versed in every branch of learning, are gifted with knowledge and good sense, and have the poise needed to serve in the royal palace. Teach these young men the language and literature of the Babylonians...They were to be trained for a three-year period, and then some of them would be made his advisers in the royal court. Daniel, Hananiah, Mishael, and Azariah were four of the young men chosen, all from the tribe of Judah. The chief official renamed them...Daniel was called Belteshazzar. Hananiah was called Shadrach. Mishael was called Meshach. Azariah was called Abednego."

They had no choice regarding whether or not they would go to Babylon – they were captured and brought there by the King's order. However, they did have a choice in terms of how they would act and behave while they were prisoners in Babylon. Their loyalty was to God alone. The decision was simple, clear and direct – no compromise or variance at any time or under any duress. It is stated and summarized in Daniel 1:8, "But Daniel resolved (purposed in his heart) that he would not defile himself with the king's food, or with the wine that he drank. Therefore he asked the chief of the eunuchs to allow him not to defile himself."

His three friends and companions were of like mind – they would not bow or bend before the king's idol. They would not compromise at any time about any matter. It was a matter of principle and commitment for these four young men. They had learned early in their lives to fear God more than any man. Even though they had been removed and transported from their home to a foreign place with different values, they would not change their physical diet or their religious custom and tradition because of a pagan king's whim or directive. There would be threats and warnings – a lion's den and a fiery furnace – but these young men were undaunted and unafraid. Their love and allegiance to God was far greater than any threat and penalty by a pagan king. Would they be respectful of the King of Babylon? Yes! Would they compromise their commitment to the God of all gods and the King of all kings? No!

What was common to these four men was their calmness during the crisis moments and their confidence in the Living God that if they did His will – He would make a way where there seemed to be no way. Daniel had to face a den of hungry lions. What will he do as they circle him and roar in a threatening manner? God made it possible for Daniel to sleep peacefully in the midst of danger. It reminds one of the words of David in Psalm 3:5, "I lay down and slept; I woke again, for the Lord sustained me." David also utters similar words in Psalm 4:8, "In peace I will both lie down and sleep; for you alone, O Lord, make me dwell in safety." It's the tranquil spirit that the Lord grants to sustain one in the midst of any storm of life or pending danger. It's what Jesus said (John 14:27): "My Peace I leave with you – My Peace I give unto you. Let not your heart be troubled, neither let it be afraid."

When Daniel's friends had to face the reality of a blazing fire in the furnace – all because they refused to bow before the king's image – their calmness and confidence remained steadfast. Just before they are to be thrown into the furnace, there is this exchange with the king – Daniel 3:15-18, "Now if you are ready when you hear the sound of the horn, pipe, lyre, harp, bagpipe, and every kind of music, to fall down and worship the image that I have made, well and good. But if you do not worship, you shall immediately be cast into a burning fiery furnace. And who is the god who will deliver you out of my hands? Shadrach, Meshach, and Abednego answered and said to the king, O Nebuchadnezzar, we have no need to answer you in this matter. If this be so, our God whom we serve is able to deliver us from the burning fiery furnace, and he will deliver us out of your hand, O king. But if not, be it known to you, O king, that we will not serve your gods or worship the golden image that you have set up."

They are simply stating that (a) there is not a threat so great, (b) no intimidation so strong, and (c) there is no fire so hot to cause them to compromise their faith, trust and confidence in The One and Only True and Living God. The words are stirring: "...our God whom we serve is able to deliver us from the burning fiery furnace, and he will deliver us out of your hand, O king." The fact is that God is able to deliver. The faith is that God will deliver. Do you believe that great truth – Our God is able and He will deliver us...? Is that fundamental to your walk of faith and the commitment you have made to the Lord Jesus Christ. Is you Christianity a matter of convenience or one of commitment? There is a considerable difference – one needs to be hot or cold – lukewarm us unacceptable to the Lord Jesus Christ.

A fourth example is Paul and Silas. In Acts 16:9-10, "And a vision appeared to Paul in the night: a man of Macedonia was standing there, urging him and saying, Come over to Macedonia and help us. And when Paul had seen the vision, immediately we sought to go on into Macedonia, concluding that God had called us to preach the gospel to them."

As they set out on this journey, they come to Philippi, which is a leading city of the district of Macedonia and a Roman colony. They encounter Lydia who is part of a small prayer group of women. The chapter indicates: "The Lord opened her heart to pay attention to what was said by Paul." They also encounter a slave girl "who had a spirit of divination and brought her owners much gain by fortune-telling." This becomes a very defining moment for Paul and his companions. Paul casts out the spirit of divination from the slave girl. The result is stated in Acts 16:19-24, "But when her owners saw that their hope of gain was gone, they seized Paul and Silas and dragged them into the marketplace before the rulers. And when they had brought them to the magistrates, they said, These men are Jews, and they are disturbing our city. They advocate customs that are not lawful for us as Romans to accept or practice. The crowd joined in attacking them, and the magistrates tore the garments off them and gave orders to beat them with rods. And when they had inflicted many blows upon them, they threw them into prison, ordering the jailer to keep them safely. Having received this order, he put them into the inner prison and fastened their feet in the stocks."

Their best effort for the Lord is now thwarted. The vision Paul had received cannot be met and realized. They are fastened securely in a prison. Their freedom to proclaim the Gospel is now denied. What should one do in such a predicament? How can one reason with the unreasonable? Paul had been annoyed by the slave girl but being in a maximum security situation is even more annoying. How can the task of ministry be carried out? What is the purpose of the vision, journey and effort – to spend time in jail – incarcerated – told not to disturb the city? One should never jump to conclusions or get ahead of God's plans and purposes. In Acts 16:25-26, we see God's purposes begin to unfold - "About midnight Paul and Silas were praying and singing hymns to God, and the prisoners were listening to them, and suddenly there was a great earthquake, so that the foundations of the prison were shaken. And immediately all the doors were opened, and everyone's bonds were unfastened."

Who would've guessed this would or could occur? How could this have been anticipated or expected? What does it mean for them immediately or ultimately? Very quickly, they find out exactly what it means. The Jailer is ready to kill himself and Paul yells out to him – Don't! Wait! We're all still here! No one has tried to escape! Then – in Acts 16:29-32, we read: "And the jailer called for lights and rushed in, and trembling with fear he fell down before Paul and Silas. Then he brought them out and said, Sirs, what must I do to be saved? And they said, Believe in the Lord Jesus, and you will be saved, you and your household. And they spoke the word of the Lord to him and to all who were in his house."

Their mission is now back on track. The Gospel can now be proclaimed once again. People are hearing and responding to the Gospel. A Church will soon be started in Philippi – a Church to which Paul would write and say, Philippians 1:3-6 - "I thank my God in all my remembrance of you, always in every prayer of mine for you all making my prayer with joy, because of your partnership in the gospel from the first day until now. And I am sure of this, that he who began a good work in you will bring it to completion at the day of Jesus Christ."

Another example is Jesus Christ. This brief summary is given in I Peter 2:21-25, "Christ also suffered for you, leaving you an example, so that you might follow in his steps. He committed no sin, neither was deceit found in his mouth. When he was reviled, he did not revile in return; when he suffered, he did not threaten, but continued entrusting himself to him who judges justly. He himself bore our sins in his body on the tree, that we might die to sin and live to righteousness. By his wounds you have been healed. For you were straying like sheep, but have now returned to the Shepherd and Overseer of your souls."

Jesus left us an example in many ways. In Philippians 2, as He took on the form of a servant and humbled Himself and became obedient unto death... In John 13 as he assumed the role of the servant and washed the feet of His disciples as an example and demonstration of His love... In Matthew 4 as He set the example on how one can and should resist temptation by making use of the Holy Scriptures to rebuke the devil... In Luke 24:42, as He yielded completely to all of what the Father's will was for Him – "Father, if you are willing, remove this cup from me. Nevertheless, not my will, but yours, be done."

Thee are many examples of godly people in the Scriptures. One gets an idea of some of them by reading Hebrews 11. The writer shares the limitation in giving a brief summary or vignette of all who could be references when he states in Hebrews 11:32-34, "And what more shall I say? For time would fail me to tell of Gideon, Barak, Samson, Jephthah, of David and Samuel and the prophets - who through faith conquered kingdoms, enforced justice, obtained promises, stopped the mouths of lions, quenched the power of fire, escaped the edge of the sword, were made strong out of weakness, became mighty in war, put foreign armies to flight...."

There are sufficient people of faith recorded in God's Word who could be chosen as an example for one's life. There are outstanding women, such as Ruth, Esther, Abigail, Phoebe, Lydia, Eunice and Lois. There are other men and women tucked away in Scripture that could be chosen as a model – Simeon and Barnabas are among others that come readily to mind – such as, Nathan and Obadiah. There is Mary, the Mother of Jesus, and Anna in the Temple. Search the Scriptures – there are several examples - you'll find them and learn from each of them.

Personal Study Questions - - -

What is basic and essential for one to be an example that you would be willing to follow?

What characteristics should you possess if you wanted to be an example to others?

What should you purpose to develop in your life as an example – prayer; the fruit of the Spirit; a committed life; a life free from compromise?

If you could select some Biblical person that you would want to be like (other than Jesus Christ), who would you choose? Why?

Great Forgiveness

If you confess with your mouth that Jesus is Lord and believe in your heart that God raised him from the dead, you will be saved. For with the heart one believes and is justified, and with the mouth one confesses and is saved.
Romans 10:9-10

All of us have the sense of having done something that was unacceptable and wrong during our lifetime. As a child and in one's youth, discipline was administered in one way or another and it was obvious that punishment was being meted out for some negative behavior or an unseemly comment. When people speak of "the good old days", they probably aren't referring to the time when one's mouth was washed out with laundry detergent soap or Lifebuoy Soap (I wish my Mother and Grandmother had chosen Ivory Soap instead) because of a "dirty" word spoken or a disrespectful comment made. For too many ("in the good old days"), their theme song might've been: "I'm Forever Blowing – Bubbles..." At some point, one wants to eliminate the soap taste; or come out of the corner in which he has been standing; or be able to play with his friends once again; or be able to have a dessert or treat. Punishment and penalty is never a pleasant experience. One will promise almost anything just so long as the penalty is lifted and the punishment has come to an end. As children, we didn't comprehend the meaning or idea of forgiveness – we just knew that we were no longer being punished for what we had done. It would be many years before any comprehension or knowledge of forgiveness would begin to be discerned and understood.

To begin to understand what it is to be forgiven, one must learn what it is and means to forgive. To forgive means: "to grant pardon for or remission of an offense; to grant pardon to a person; to cease to feel resentment against: to forgive one's enemies; to cancel an indebtedness or liability of; to pardon an offense or an offender..." A negative action taken or comment spoken about or to another individual can cause a deep mental or emotional wound for the other person. It causes another person to feel unwanted, unneeded and/or unaccepted.

The Mayo Clinic Staff has produced an interesting discussion about forgiveness. Some of the Staff Comments includes: "When someone you care about hurts you, you can hold on to anger, resentment and thoughts of revenge - or embrace forgiveness and move forward." The study is entitled: "Forgiveness: Letting Go of Grudges and Bitterness." Katherine Piderman, Ph.D., staff chaplain at Mayo Clinic, Rochester, Minnesota discusses forgiveness and how it can lead you down the path of physical, emotional and spiritual well-being. She summarizes: "Nearly everyone has been hurt by the actions or words of another. Perhaps your mother criticized your parenting skills or your partner had an affair. These wounds can leave you with lasting feelings of anger, bitterness and even vengeance — but if you don't practice forgiveness, you may be the one who pays most dearly. By embracing forgiveness, you embrace peace, hope, gratitude and joy."

She asks and answers the question: "What is forgiveness? Generally, forgiveness is a decision to let go of resentment and thoughts of revenge. The act that hurt or offended you may always remain a part of your life, but forgiveness can lessen its grip on you and help you focus on other, positive parts of your life. Forgiveness can even lead to feelings of understanding, empathy and compassion for the one who hurt you. Forgiveness doesn't mean that you deny the other person's responsibility for hurting you, and it doesn't minimize or justify the wrong. You can forgive the person without excusing the act. Forgiveness brings a kind of peace that helps you go on with life. Letting go of grudges and bitterness makes way for compassion, kindness and peace...It is easy to hold a grudge when you're hurt by someone you love and trust...If you dwell on hurtful events or situations, grudges filled with resentment, vengeance and hostility may take root. If you allow negative feelings to crowd out positive feelings, you may find yourself swallowed up by your own bitterness or sense of injustice...Forgiveness is a commitment to a process of change. A way to begin is by recognizing the value of forgiveness and its importance in your life...Then reflect on the facts of the situation, how you've reacted, and how this combination has affected your life, health and well-being. When you're ready, actively choose to forgive the person who's offended you. Move away from your role as victim and release the control and power the offending person and situation have had in your life...

"As you let go of grudges, you'll no longer define your life by how you've been hurt. You may even find compassion and understanding...If the hurtful event involved someone whose relationship you otherwise value, forgiveness may lead to reconciliation..." She goes one step further: "What if I'm the one who needs forgiveness?" Her answer: "Consider admitting the wrong you've done to those you've harmed, speaking of your sincere sorrow or regret, and specifically asking for forgiveness — without making excuses. Remember, however, you can't force someone to forgive you. Others need to move to forgiveness in their own time. Simply acknowledge your faults and admit your mistakes, then commit to treating others with compassion, empathy and respect."

From a strict Biblical position, the prayer taught to the disciples by Jesus Christ (The Lord's Prayer – Matthew 6:12) contains these words: "and forgive us our debts, as we also have forgiven our debtors." The New Living Translation is: "and forgive us our sins, just as we have forgiven those who have sinned against us." It's the reciprocal act of forgiveness and has in mind the words that immediately follow The Lord's Prayer – Matthew 6:14-15, "For if you forgive others their trespasses, your heavenly Father will also forgive you, but if you do not forgive others their trespasses, neither will your Father forgive your trespasses." The words recorded in Luke 11:4 vary slightly when Luke records: "and forgive us our sins, for we ourselves forgive everyone who is indebted to us." The New Living Translation has: "And forgive us our sins -- just as we forgive those who have sinned against us."

The two elements of the prayer are (a) inward reflection, confession and seeking forgiveness for personal offenses and sins, and (b) outward reflection, the act of forgiving others and seeking reconciliation unconditionally. The inward confession is of great benefit in one's relationship with the Lord. While it is repentance on the one hand, it is restoration of fellowship with the Lord – a personal renewal and revitalization. It is difficult to hear and try to understand the one who allows, "I may forgive – but – I'll never forget..." There needs to be the understanding and practice of the Lord's ways and means of forgiveness which is established in Psalm 103:12 (NIV), "as far as the east is from the west, so far has he removed our transgressions from us." It also includes the covenantal words of Hebrews 10:16-17 (ESV), "This is the covenant that I will make with them after those days, declares the Lord: I will put my laws on their hearts, and write them on their minds, then he adds, I will remember their sins and their lawless deeds no more." What a tremendous concept and act of mercy – God removes our transgressions from us and pledges to no longer remember our sins and lawless deeds. If this is one's expectation and hope in terms of God in His relationship and acts toward man, should ours be any less than His in our relationship and acts with one another? It would be best if one's response is an emphatic – "No!"

It is interesting that the Mayo Clinic Staff study addresses "Forgiveness: Letting go of grudges and bitterness." One of the major areas for one's attention in his Christian walk includes the same areas, along with others. The reason is the spiritual import for and impact upon one's spiritual growth and development. Additionally, it involves an attitude and action in terms of the Holy Spirit. Paul states it clearly in Ephesians 4:30-32, "And do not grieve the Holy Spirit of God, by whom you were sealed for the day of redemption. Let all bitterness and wrath and anger and clamor and slander be put away from you, along with all malice. Be kind to one another, tenderhearted, forgiving one another, as God in Christ forgave you."

It is a fact that bitterness, wrath, anger, clamor, slander, rage, grudges not only impact one spiritually but it can have a devastating effect on one both physically and psychologically as well. Wrath, anger and rage can and will elevate one's blood pressure and have a harmful result in terms of one's cardio-vascular health. In this one area alone, it should be easy to see how harmful this can be for one's physical well-being, and mental health. The Amplified Bible translates Ephesians 4:31, "Let all bitterness and indignation and wrath (passion, rage, bad temper) and resentment (anger, animosity) and quarreling (brawling, clamor, contention) and slander (evil-speaking, abusive or blasphemous language) be banished from you, with all malice (spite, ill will, or baseness of any kind)."

There is very sound Biblical counsel in terms of anger, wrath, rage and bitterness. In Psalm 37:1, 8 – "Fret not...Refrain from anger, and forsake wrath! Fret not yourself; it tends only to evil." The Message paraphrase is: "Don't bother your head with braggarts or wish you could succeed like the wicked...Bridle your anger, trash your wrath, cool your pipes - it only makes things worse." The New Living Translation is: "Don't worry about the wicked. Don't envy those who do wrong...Stop your anger! Turn from your rage!"

The focus is that one must not allow for anger, wrath, rage and bitterness. It is an area that needs and requires immediate attention. One needs to move from the stress of anger and rage to both peace and rest in the Lord. There is no substitute for the calm and gentle spirit. It is a fact that one's disobedience to God's best intention for mankind – to know and practice forgiveness – grieves the Holy Spirit of God. It is too easy in a secular-oriented society and culture to ignore that our actions and behavior are not without consequences. We need only to recall God's observation and declaration regarding the behavior of mankind in the days of Noah.

The crucial words are recorded in Genesis 6:5-6, "The Lord saw that the wickedness of man was great in the earth, and that every intention of the thoughts of his heart was only evil continually. And the Lord was sorry that he had made man on the earth, and it grieved him to his heart." Once again the word "grieve" appears. It means "to feel grief or great sorrow; to distress mentally." The text shares with us how the heart of God is impacted and affected by the indifference and disobedience of mankind – He is "sorry" and "it grieved Him to His heart."

In a similar way, Jesus reminds His followers in the Olivet Discourse, that the same type of attitude and response will be observed just before the Judgment of God becomes the reality in the last days. This is recorded in Matthew 24:37-39, "For as were the days of Noah, so will be the coming of the Son of Man. For as in those days before the flood they were eating and drinking, marrying and giving in marriage, until the day when Noah entered the ark, and they were unaware until the flood came and swept them all away, so will be the coming of the Son of Man." If the behavior of mankind is similar, what do you suppose is occurring in terms of the heart of God? It would be very safe to conclude that God is impacted in the same way by the indifference and disobedience of mankind – and - He is "sorry" and "it grieves Him to His heart."

It seems as though a broad consideration of forgiveness that includes confession and repentance, we somehow have lost sight of and neglected contrition. The idea is that one needs to have and show a "sincere penitence or remorse…or sorrow for and detestation of sin." It is a sorrow borne out of – not having been caught and deemed guilty – but one gaining a sense of the gravity of sin and having a detestation of it. This would especially be more intense if and when a person has the realization that sin – either one or many – is an offense to God and necessitated a blood sacrifice to make atonement for that one sin or many sins. This is conveyed in Hebrews 9:18-22, "…For when every commandment of the law had been declared by Moses to all the people, he took the blood of calves and goats and…sprinkled both the book itself and all the people, saying, This is the blood of the covenant that God commanded for you…Indeed, under the law almost everything is purified with blood, and without the shedding of blood there is no forgiveness (no remission) of sins."

It is the same thought and idea stated by Paul in Ephesians 1:7-8, "In him (Christ) we have redemption through his blood, the forgiveness of our trespasses and sins, according to the riches of his grace, which he lavished upon us…" Since something, and ultimately someone had to die and shed blood because of one's individual sin, it should cause one to be brokenhearted because his sin necessitated such a price and penalty. This is how and why contrition - "a sincere penitence or remorse…a sorrow for and detestation of sin" - is the intense reality as one confesses his/her sin and seeks cleansing from it and forgiveness for it.

There are two obvious illustrations of contrition that can be of help to us. The first is in the companion Psalms – Psalm 32 and Psalm 51 – where David looks at himself as God is looking at him and realizes he has committed and is guilty of a heinous act before a Holy God. It is the lustful desire for another man's wife; the committing of adultery and impregnation of Bathsheba; the ultimate murder of her husband Uriah in the attempt to cover up his negative behavior; his confrontation by Nathan the prophet (II Samuel 12:1-23) – all leading to his restlessness of spirit and growing conviction because of his sinful acts.

These are the acts and events that lead up to his saying in Psalm 32:1-5, "Blessed is the one whose transgression is forgiven, whose sin is covered. Blessed is the man against whom the Lord counts no iniquity, and in whose spirit there is no deceit. For when I kept silent, my bones wasted away through my groaning all day long. For day and night your hand was heavy upon me; my strength was dried up as by the heat of summer. I acknowledged my sin to you, and I did not cover my iniquity; I said, I will confess my transgressions to the Lord, and you forgave the iniquity of my sin."

The process of his confession, repentance and contrition also included his conclusions expressed in Psalm 51:1-4, "Have mercy on me, O God, according to your steadfast love; according to your abundant mercy blot out my transgressions. Wash me thoroughly from my iniquity, and cleanse me from my sin! For I know my transgressions, and my sin is ever before me. Against you, you only, have I sinned and done what is evil in your sight..." Day and night his sin gnawed at him and drove him to the decision and action to deal with his sin and to get back into a right relationship with the Lord. It could not be covered up and could no longer be avoided. The conviction came when he came to the moment of realization that his sin was against God – His holiness and His Word. This drove him to the point in his prayer of saying: "Against you, you only, have I sinned and done what is evil in your sight...

In Psalm 51:9-12 his pleading before God and his desire for a full measure of God's mercy is seen when he prays, "Hide your face from my sins, and blot out all my iniquities. Create in me a clean heart, O God, and renew a right spirit within me. Cast me not away from your presence, and take not your Holy Spirit from me. Restore to me the joy of your salvation, and uphold me with a willing spirit." The weight and burden of sin is heavy and debilitating. It has to be removed and can only occur as it is confessed. While most tend to delay, this is a case where "the sooner, the better" principle should most definitely be applied. David had tried to avoid admitting his sin – but finally – sought cleansing and forgiveness by God.

The second illustration appears in Luke 15:18-24 – The Parable of the Prodigal Son. In terms of the Gospel, it's similar to how all are before they seek forgiveness and cleansing in and through Jesus Christ. The confession and contrition is succinct and sufficient. Note the decision reached and the action taken by the prodigal son, "I will arise and go to my father, and I will say to him, Father, I have sinned against heaven and before you. I am no longer worthy to be called your son. Treat me as one of your hired servants. And he arose and came to his father. But while he was still a long way off, his father saw him and felt compassion, and ran and embraced him and kissed him. And the son said to him, Father, I have sinned against heaven and before you. I am no longer worthy to be called your son. But the father said to his servants, Bring quickly the best robe, and put it on him, and put a ring on his hand, and shoes on his feet. And bring the fattened calf and kill it, and let us eat and celebrate. For this my son was dead, and is alive again; he was lost, and is found. And they began to celebrate."

The contrition aspect is seen in his willingness to come back into relationship with his father as a servant rather than as the demanding son who left in his arrogance and with an independent spirit. He left – not caring about the shame and loss this cost his father – but as one wanting to do his thing in his way. He went away with pride and now he is returning with penitence; he went away with all of his possessions and now he is returning with poverty; he went away dressed like a prince and now he is returning dressed like and with the smell of a pig-sty resident. He left with his demand for his inheritance and now he is returning in humility and with a request to rejoin the father's household as a servant. Regardless of the errors in judgment made by this son, at least he retained the good sense to return to the one place where he had known love, kindness and acceptance – his father's home. He was not coming with any demands – just a humble request to be one of the servants.

In a very brief sketch of the life of John Newton, some of his background is given: "Born in England, his mother died when he was seven. His father remarried and sent him away to school for a few years. At age eleven he left school and joined his father's ship to start life as a seaman. His early years were marked by rebellion and debauchery. Newton eventually became the captain of a slave ship, but was such a cruel and vicious man, that his own crew mutinied and threw him overboard. Extracted from the waters, the slave trader himself became a slave. In 1748, while returning to England from Africa during a particularly stormy voyage, when all appeared lost, he began reading Thomas A. Kemps' book, Imitation of Christ. The message of Christ contained in this book and the frightening sea around him were used by the Holy Spirit to sow the seeds of his eventual conversion and personal acceptance of Jesus Christ as his Lord and Savior. At age eighty-two this man went home to be with his Father. Until that time he never ceased to marvel at God's mercy and grace that had so dramatically changed his life. In the last years of his life, while preaching, he proclaimed in a loud voice, My memory is nearly gone, but I remember two things: That I am a great sinner and that Christ is a great Savior!

In the Churchyard in Olney, England, you will find the name of John Newton on a tombstone. On it also you will find the following inscription written by him before his going home... "John Newton, clerk, once an infidel and libertine, a servant of slavers in Africa, was by the rich mercy of our Lord and Savior Jesus Christ, preserved, restored, pardoned, and appointed to preach the faith he had long labored to destroy.

We can understand his sense of forgiveness, restoration and acceptance when he penned in 1779 twelve stanzas to a hymn that many find and use as their own testimony. Some of the stanzas are - - -

> Amazing grace! How sweet the sound
> That saved a wretch like me!
> I once was lost, but now am found;
> Was blind, but now I see.

> 'Twas grace that taught my heart to fear,
> And grace my fears relieved;
> How precious did that grace appear
> The hour I first believed!

> Through many dangers, toils and snares,
> I have already come;
> 'Tis grace hath brought me safe thus far,
> And grace will lead me home.

Have you come to know this amazing grace, forgiveness, restoration and acceptance in the Lord Jesus Christ? Just come to Him - He will welcome you into His household.

Personal Study Questions - - -

For you, is The Lord's Prayer a meaningful act of prayer or merely a ritual used in a Worship Service?

Have you realized the importance of possessing and practicing a forgiving spirit?

Personally, how do you define forgiveness?

Great Proclamation

The Lord God has given Me The tongue of the learned, That I should know how to speak A word in season to him who is weary. He awakens Me morning by morning, He awakens My ear To hear as the learned.
Isaiah 50:4 (NKJV)

The Commission given by the Lord Jesus Christ is plain and spoken with clarity. Jesus is forthright when he states the task to be carried out – (1) proclaim the Gospel; (2) make disciples; and (3) baptize in the name of the Triune God. One would think that the clarity of the commission would cause all of the lambs and sheep of Jesus Christ to be in lockstep with each other as they march to His Orders and represent Him in the lost and dying world. What has happened between the time when the commission was first issued and today? Is the task being done adequately? Is the message being proclaimed clear or vague? There is an important question raised in Isaiah 50:10 (NKJV), "Who among you fears the Lord? Who obeys the voice of His Servant? Who walks in darkness and has no light? Let him trust in the name of the Lord and rely upon his God." This apt and timely question needs review and response.

On the Day of Pentecost in Acts 2, there was evidence of a clear understanding regarding the commission. With boldness and clarity, Peter seized the opportunity. Near the end of his sermon – Acts 2:36-42 – there is an immediate response, "Therefore let all the house of Israel know assuredly that God has made this Jesus, whom you crucified, both Lord and Christ. Now when they heard this, they were cut to the heart, and said to Peter and the rest of the apostles, Men and brethren, what shall we do? Then Peter said to them, Repent, and let every one of you be baptized in the name of Jesus Christ for the remission of sins; and you shall receive the gift of the Holy Spirit. For the promise is to you and to your children, and to all who are afar off, as many as the Lord our God will call. And with many other words he testified and exhorted them, saying, Be saved from this perverse generation. Then those who gladly received his word were baptized; and that day about three thousand souls were added to them. And they continued steadfastly in the apostles' doctrine and fellowship, in the breaking of bread, and in prayers."

Peter had preached the Gospel. When people asked what they needed to do, he stated it in one word – Repent! They would be baptized and discipleship would take place at once. The result: three thousand were added to their number and they continued with them to learn the apostle's doctrine. They entered into the fellowship opportunity and participated with those of like precious faith.

Is there any noticeable difference between the preaching on the Day of Pentecost and today? Is there any noticeable difference between the response and result on the Day of Pentecost and today? When was the last time you heard someone call out in a religious forum – "Men and brethren, what shall we do?" Could it be that the message being proclaimed today lacks the verve (great vitality, enthusiasm, and liveliness) and power Jesus promised in Acts 1:8, "But you will receive power when the Holy Spirit has come upon you, and you will be my witnesses in Jerusalem and in all Judea and Samaria, and to the end of the earth."? Most have heard that the word – power – is translated from the Greek word – dunamis – which is the root of the word dynamite. The idea is that the Word of the Gospel should and will have impact in the lives of those who hear and receive. The result that is or is not occurring today is directly connected to whether or not there is clarity in the Gospel presentation.

The first word Peter used when the question was posed – What are we to do? – was Repent! When was the last time you heard that word used in a worship service or evangelism crusade? The paraphrase in The Message of Acts 2:37-42 is: "Cut to the quick, those who were there listening asked Peter and the other apostles, Brothers! Brothers! So now what do we do? Peter said, Change your life. Turn to God and be baptized, each of you, in the name of Jesus Christ, so your sins are forgiven...He went on in this vein for a long time, urging them over and over, Get out while you can; get out of this sick and stupid culture..."

As Peter moved to Solomon's Portico, he once again had opportunity to proclaim the Gospel. His appeal to those gathered there is in Acts 3:19 (NKJV), "Repent therefore and be converted, that your sins may be blotted out, so that times of refreshing may come from the presence of the Lord..." It is stated in a straightforward manner - Repent and Be Converted, that your sins may be blotted out. As a child, we were taught a Chorus in Sunday School that conveyed this message idea spoken by Peter...

> God has blotted them out,
> I'm happy and glad and free;
> God has blotted them out –
> I'll turn to Isaiah and see:
> Chapter forty four, twenty two and three;
> He's blotted them out,
> and now I can shout - For that means me!

The word from Isaiah 44:22-23 (ESV) is, "I have blotted out your transgressions like a cloud and your sins like mist; return to me, for I have redeemed you. Sing, O heavens, for the Lord has done it; shout, O depths of the earth; break forth into singing, O mountains, O forest, and every tree in it! For the Lord has redeemed Jacob, and will be glorified in Israel."

The underlying question is still with us, namely, how can the Church today reclaim the message and power that Jesus intended when He commissioned His followers? We find ourselves almost trapped in the religious malaise (a condition of general bodily weakness or discomfort) on the one hand and personal frustration and a sense of inability to effect change on the other hand. Many of the larger churches attract people through the programs offered, the user-friendly facilities, the outlets and opportunities for use of talent, etc. There is a tendency to like and condone the entertainment and the applause that follows is not a sign of one's worship of God but appreciation for the talent displayed by the "religious performer." We have vocal and instrumental soloists; choirs singing magnificent anthems; ballet participation; orchestras with a full complement of instruments; large organs; grand pianos – and people are impressed by that presentation in a worship service.

There are "ministries" that have different emphases where the use of catch-phrases are used. One of them is a fund-raising emphasis upon "seed money" and the necessity to release your seed so God will release His harvest. In their appeal, they even resort to a negative stewardship appeal that goes something like this – "if you don't have the money now, put it on your credit card and trust God to pay-off your credit card debt."

One of the catch-phrases that has been used over the years is "Reformed and Reforming." As this chapter is being written, a letter arrived indicating that in places in South Africa the word "reformed" has caused some difficulty because "...it carries unhelpful connotations in the minds of many black Christians..." The resolve is simple – stop using that word where it is unhelpful. The Reformed Doctrines can be presented without the use of T U L I P to explain one's view in terms of Calvinism. If there is a thorough study done in the Book of Romans, all of T U L I P will become abundantly clear.

At the end of the day, for the greatest intellect or the most unlearned individual, the Gospel message that needs to be proclaimed and understood is: "Jesus loves me, this I know – for the Bible tells me so." This basic truth can be made known from John 3:16, "For God so love the world, that He gave His only-begotten Son, that whosoever believeth in Him, should not perish but have everlasting life." An additional verse that conveys this same thought is I John 4:9-10, "In this the love of God was made manifest among us, that God sent his only Son into the world, so that we might live through him. In this is love, not that we have loved God but that he loved us and sent his Son to be the propitiation for our sins." The word "propitiation" means God's Divine wrath was satisfied in the death of His Son for our sins.

While sitting in a Seminary class one day, the learned Professor was lecturing on the atonement of Christ and what that means for one who has neither set a foot in a church nor attended a religious institution of any kind. The Professor told of his effort to share the Gospel with a young man who had questions for which he thought he needed answers. After a period of time, the kindly Professor said to the young man: "If I could answer all the questions you pose to your satisfaction, would you then be ready to receive Jesus Christ as your Savior and Lord?"

The lesson the Professor wanted us to learn was the need to keep one's eye on the ball. There may be – will be – much racket and distraction – just remember your task and mission and don't get side-tracked from it. The Church and professing Christian people need to remember that truth – remember your task and mission – and – don't listen to the noise or let yourself become distracted in any way.

In a past church affiliation, the church had an outdoor evangelistic meeting on the Boardwalk. One concession operator became so annoyed with the preaching of the Gospel that whenever a speaker got up to take his turn preaching, the concessionaire would turn up his amplifier and spew all kinds of talk and clamor as his way to interrupt the effort of those endeavoring to preach the Gospel. Some were perplexed and decided to go home or try some other time. It was their choice and decision and that is what they did. The error in that thinking was the presentation of the Gospel is not just by a preacher standing on a soap box or soda crate.

Some remained and began to hand out Gospels of John and Gospel Tracts. This opened up opportunities to speak one on one with different individuals. The Concession Operator could do anything he wanted – but – he could not prevent the Gospel from being shared. The Gospel is unrestricted in terms of a format used to present it. The words written in I Peter 3:15 are so meaningful. Peter – the one who so boldly made known the Gospel on the Day of Pentecost – is writing to the persecuted Church and tells the believers: "but in your hearts honor Christ the Lord as holy, always being prepared to make a defense to anyone who asks you for a reason for the hope that is in you; yet do it with gentleness and respect..." The same Gospel but a different tactic.

The words of Peter convey a similar thought Paul shared as his testimony and commitment to ministry in Romans 1:16, "For I am not ashamed of the gospel, for it is the power of God for salvation to everyone who believes, to the Jew first and also to the Greek." There will be all kinds of situations and circumstances that arise in one's lifetime. Wherever one is and whatever the circumstance may be, do not be ashamed of the Gospel – but - always be prepared to offer a reason for the hope that is in you. It is to be done with gentleness and respect but it must always be done without fear. In I Peter 3:14, Peter wrote: "But even if you should suffer for righteousness' sake, you will be blessed. Have no fear of them, nor be troubled..." Have no fear! The Psalmist would add: "Serve the Lord with gladness." This is our opportunity and privilege for our Lord.

Personal Study Questions - - -

Do you have a clear statement that you can give, your reason, for the hope that is in you? Can you share that succinctly? How and where would you begin?

If you were in the World Trade Center as it was about to collapse and you had just a minute or less to answer someone's question: "What do I have to do to be saved?", what answer would you give in that brief moment?

What Scripture Verse would you use in the above situation? Do you know, and could you recite Acts 16:31 and/or Romans 10:13?

If you wanted to practice giving a succinct presentation of the Gospel, what or where are some of the places where you can try and do this? Do you know how to begin the conversation about the Gospel?

Would you be comfortable to try this question and approach: "If you were to die today and enter into the presence of God, and He would say to you - _____ why should I let you into my heaven, what would you say?

May God give you the desire and necessary confidence as you share His Gospel with those all-around you!

Concluding Thoughts

Early in my youth, the Sunday School Class was made to memorize and recite Proverbs 14:12, "There is a way that seems right to a man, but its end is the way to death." Some thought they would pull a fast one on the Teacher by giving the reference as Proverbs 16:25. The Teacher was way ahead of the class and knew the identical wording occurs in both texts. He reminded us that since we noted the two references that we should never forget the words of the text and to always choose God's way for our lives.

The Chapters of this book serve as a reminder of the life that is possible for one to live, and to make us aware of the snares that would sidetrack us from the best course for our lives. The closing Chapters focus on the Shepherd, the Example and Forgiveness – placed there to help us to stay on the right course and not to stray away from the Shepherd's side.

It is my hope that these Chapters will serve as a reminder of truths you've already learned and dangers that you must continue to avoid. May you always be strong in the Lord and in the strength of His might!

ABOUT THE AUTHOR

James Perry was born and reared in Brooklyn, NY and lived there for the first twenty years of his life. During his teenage years he had opportunity of being involved in street corner meetings and outdoor evangelism. It entailed providing music and the distribution of Gospel Tracts. Later on, he was able to be part of a team that did Prison Ministry. Once again, it was mostly providing music and occasionally being asked to give a testimony.

In the providence of God, he went to work at Lakeside Bible Conference in Carmel, NY and was given the responsibility of working with teenage boys from the inner-city of New York. It was a visionary ministry that had many positive results. He roomed in a two-man cabin with one who was the President of the Student Body of Columbia Bible College (now Columbia International University) in Columbia, SC. This roommate was persistent throughout the summer as he asked him repeatedly whether or not he knew God's purpose and will for his life.

At the end of the summer, he rode to Columbia, SC with some friends who had previously enrolled in Columbia Bible College,. His thought was that he would hitch-hike back home after classes began for the Fall Semester. The Lord had other plans for his life and he was allowed to enroll and begin studying for the ministry there from 1954-57. He completed his College work at Covenant College, now located at Lookout Mountain, GA and went on to Covenant Theological Seminary in St. Louis, MO and completed that training in 1964.

Part of the Lord's plan for his life was to bring a young woman into his life during his freshman year. They were united in marriage in 1956 and have been partners in ministry from that point of time onward. The Lord has given him and his wife, Peggy, four children, fourteen grand-children, and four great-grandchildren.

He has served as Pastor for more almost forty-seven years in churches from New Jersey to Colorado to Alabama - with some in-between - and has had great joy in doing so.

It is his hope that some of the lessons he has learned along the way, as well as some of his teaching over the years, will be a practical help in this written form.

May the Lord bless and enrich you as you study His Word and walk in His ways.